And You, Who Do You Say I Am?

Other Christopher Books

Young Ideas
Articles written by young people

Enjoy the Lord
A guide to prayer

Three Minutes a Day
Volume 20 in a series of daily meditations

What a Day This Can Be!
A "Three Minutes" book

Bits and Pieces
A treasury of Christopher quotes

You Can Still Change the World
Techniques for improving society

Also Available: Christopher Conversations cassettes, and bulk copies of Christopher News Notes. For full descriptive material, write to: The Christophers, 12 East 48 St., New York, NY 10017

And You, Who Do You Say I Am?

Matthew 16:15

Collected by
Catherine de Vinck

With a Foreword by
Father John Catoir

THE CHRISTOPHERS, 12 East 48th St., New York 10017

Table of Contents

Foreword

Father John Catoir
Director, The Christophers

How would you react if you were asked to put in writing your deepest feelings about Jesus Christ? It would be a challenge, wouldn't it?

Well that's precisely how this book came to be written. Catherine de Vinck presented this question to a number of her friends and acquaintances: "For you, who is Jesus Christ?" Some of them responded within a few days, some took weeks, others months. There were various degrees of joy and discomfort with the assignment, but nearly everyone accepted it. (She took a couple of the essays from interviews carried on our TV program, *Christopher Closeup.*)

Catherine de Vinck is a mother, a well-known poet, and a woman of great charm. She is well acquainted with the intricacies of language and when she asked the contributors to share with her, and with us, their intimate thoughts about the Lord, she knew she was asking a great deal.

Our lived experience tells us what a rare and beautiful thing friendship can be. We know too that Jesus gave the word "friendship" a special meaning when He said, "No longer do I call you servants . . . but I have called you friends" (John 15:15). The word "friend" has been used indiscriminately over the years and its meaning has been diluted. "I have called you beloved," might be a better translation of Jesus' words.

The mystery of one's personal relationship with Jesus is not easy to express, but it does make for fascinating reading. The following series of essays are all different, and yet all very much the same. Some of them are like private love letters, others simple statements of fact, but each one is a self-revelation. We believe the book is of immense value in revealing the mystery of God's love which is very much alive in the world today.

In reading, we suggest that you take one or two at a time, comparing them with your own thoughts and, where appropriate, using them as a springboard for prayer.

We hope you enjoy them.

Introduction

Catherine de Vinck

"When Jesus came to the region of Caesarea Philippi, He put this question to His disciples: 'Who do people say the Son of Man is?' And they replied, 'Some say He is John the Baptist, some Elijah and others Jeremiah or one of the prophets.' 'And you,' He continued, 'who do you say I am?'

Then Simon Peter spoke up: 'You are the Christ,' he said, 'the Son of the Living God'."

Matthew 16:13-17

The same question is asked of every person today. In fact, it is the central and most demanding question, for its answer shapes our daily lives, clarifies not only who Jesus is, but also who we are.

If, like Peter, we too proclaim Jesus to be the Christ, the Son of the Living God, this acknowledgment radically alters our lives. Jesus tells us that if we belong to Him, we are born anew, not of flesh and blood, but of the Spirit. No longer can we blindly endorse "the ways of the world." Our thoughts, our values, our deeds must be illuminated by the teachings of the One who calls himself the Way, the Truth and the Life.

I have asked many friends (and a few other people whom I only know indirectly) for testimonies of their

faith; I have put that hard question to them: "For you,
who is Jesus Christ? who do you say He is?"

Many of those who answered thanked me for the
opportunity to express their faith. A priest wrote, "I am
delighted you asked me because writing this testimony
focused my heart. It is so lovely to know that even if
I am sinful and distracted, Jesus is my joy!" A woman
said, "It is the kind of challenge that leads to important
soul-searching. And I welcome it."

Only a few turned down the assignment—and when
they did, it was graciously and for very sound reasons.
A middle-aged man wrote, "My own spirituality is not
gaited for any sort of articulation. It is just not something I could ever talk about without a great deal of
stammer and muddle." Another friend wrote, "I pon-
dered the question carefully but have an inner reluc-
tance to answer it. It is such a personal and delicate
thing for me that I feel it cannot be expressed."

The most moving refusal came from a young woman
whose vocation is to serve the poor. She told me that
recently she was walking through the Bowery in New
York with a nurse, ready to provide first-aid for the
drunk and sick destitutes on the streets. A young man
came to her, holding out his open hand: the palm had
a deep bleeding wound. The young woman cleaned and
bandaged it. Before telling me this story, she had ex-
cused herself, asking me to forgive her for not writing
a testimony. "I cannot write very well," she told me,
"and what could I say? . . ." She is one of the blessed
"little ones" who are pure of heart and will see God.

I am very grateful to all those who have responded

so generously and openly. They have given witness to Jesus as the Lord of their lives; they have spoken, not from the viewpoint of intellectual knowledge, but from the passion of their hearts—for ultimately this is how we know Jesus best. Even if our minds have the right theological answers, it is through the heart, through love that we encounter Jesus.

I do not deny the necessity of rational enquiry, nor do I wish to imply that the mind is merely a cold instrument incapable of fiery ardor, but it does seem to me that faith is an affair of the heart. We love father, mother, spouse, children, friends, not because we have applied our minds to the study of parenthood, marriage or friendship: we love through the heart—but this does not mean blindly and without cause.

Jacques Maritain wrote somewhere: "Faith opens a thousand eyes in the heart." Through the spirit of love, we "see" what a hundred years of persevering studies could not let us perceive: we see that Jesus is the Lord.

After the Resurrection, when Jesus appeared to His disciples, they were frightened. He said to them, "Look at my hands and feet, see and touch for yourselves" (Luke 24:39).

See and *touch*. The people who wrote this book—for it is their book, not mine—have *seen* and *touched;* they have experienced the actuality of Jesus; they know that here and now He is present with abiding power.

The Incarnation is not merely an historical event, a temporary breakthrough, a momentary epiphany of God-with-us: "I am with you always, yes, to the end of time." These are the concluding words of the Gospel of Matthew. The promise is not vague, abstract, spiritual: it has to do with our human ways and immediate personal needs, with the shape and direction of our lives: *See* and *touch!*

In order to identify Himself, Jesus shows the wounds in His hands and feet. He tells us He is our brother, a wounded Man who shares our pain. Yet at the same time He is present to us in power and glory. He lifts us out of the jaws of death and lets us see and touch and taste what it means to participate already now in the resurrection.

We often speak of our "search" for God, we seek Him out, we reach out—out, as if He were light-years away from our concerns. But He has found us, touched us, made Himself accessible to us through Jesus His Son. We do not need intellectual acrobatics to meet Him: He communicates Himself to us through Jesus in a simple way that follows the rhythm of our daily existence.

The Word was made flesh in Bethlehem of Judah almost two thousand years ago in the person of Jesus, the Son of Mary. But He is the same yesterday, today and tomorrow: he is God-with-us, forming and reforming the community of Christians into a community of love.

The creation of this community does not happen all at once: often we are intractable, we resist the work of the Spirit, we tear apart the seamless robe of Christ. Yet, we have this hope, this vision, that the Kingdom of God will come about, that already now it is prefigured and seen—if only as through a glass, darkly. Already our eyes are open and our hearts burn with love, and we recognize Him, Christ our Lord, at the Breaking of the Bread.

I have gathered the following testimonies in the hope that many people will read them, look into their own hearts, and ponder the question Christ Himself is asking: "Who do you say the Son of Man is?" May all answer with Peter, "You are the Christ, the Son of the Living God!"

Do We See Him?

Kathleen Leis

Jesus Christ comes to life in His people on earth. Several months ago, struggling to express my feelings about Him, I was moved to write the following, which is as close as I can come to telling you who Jesus is to me.

Do We See Him

In the tiny black body, belly distended with malnutrition, match-stick legs and arms?
"I was hungry, and you fed Me."

In the defiant young girl, thirsting for love?
"Thirsty, and you gave Me to drink."

In the uncertain, lost expression of a mentally retarded adult?
"I was a stranger, and you received Me in your home."

In the old lady, shivering in a thin, ragged sweater, her lips blue with cold?
"Naked, and you clothed Me."

In the drunken man, stumbling along the curb?

"I was sick, and you took care of Me."

In the hopeless face of the man behind bars?
"In prison, and you visited Me."

Do we see *Him?*

"And the King said, 'I tell you indeed, whenever you did this for one of the least important of these brothers of mine, you did it for me!' "

Kathleen Leis, a former ballet dancer, is now a homemaker in Riverside, Conn., and is head of the Committee for Social Concern for the Diocese of Bridgeport.

My Life in Jesus

Marie E. Ged

As far back as I can remember, I questioned God: "Why was I born?" I was sure there was a reason, and that He had a purpose in mind when He created me.

Throughout my school years, I had been taught the fear of God, eternal punishment and doom by the strictest of Sisters. In my heart, I just couldn't picture a God like that! My God was much gentler, kinder and more forgiving.

Yet, in the course of my growing years, I could not eliminate the notion of God's wrath that had been drummed into my head. I read incessantly, trying to find answers; I attended novenas and believed the papal blessing could counteract any wrong I had committed. I recited the rosary every day and recorded every good deed, hoping God would also be keeping accounts. I spent part of every Saturday afternoon cooped up in a closed confessional, and never missed Mass on Sundays. But all this wasn't enough: I felt nothing, and wanted to feel something substantial about the God I was speaking to.

The confusion continued into high school, then into my marriage. I questioned everything and everybody, searching in my heart for an answer. "Who is my God, and why did He make me?" From my Baltimore Catechism, I could remember only one answer. "God made me to know, love and serve Him." Who? Why? How can I serve someone so invisible? I needed something substantial, a reason and purpose to fulfill.

Then my husband was in a car accident. He had to go through three spinal operations in three years before he could walk again. Our marriage was being built on blocks of loyalty, patience and perseverance. We had grown, and felt our faith had pulled us through. But God had other ideas. We were to be tested again and again, until we became what we were supposed to be.

Every personal struggle, every tragic situation, every perilous decision I had to make was only a rung on the ladder. Building on my experience, accepting my part in the plan, and seeing the ultimate outcome were all for a reason: that I could make some small contribution to others.

As I look back now, I realize God used me as an instrument. At the time, I could find no reason for my suffering and heartbreak. "Why," I questioned, "did my husband leave me?" What had I done wrong to deserve the curious stares and questions from people in my family and community? Eight months later, he came back home—a man transformed by the hand of Jesus.

What did it all mean? He never stopped loving me, so why did he go? The time he spent away, I know now, was a time of soul-searching, repentance, and a way of learning about himself and his relationship to his God.

Through it all, we both learned a lot. But I never realized how much others had gained from our experience. I never knew that through all this, they were watching our reactions for signs of anger, resentment or

loss of faith. Yes, we were being used as examples for
others.

For the last six years now, my husband and I have
been carrying out our apostolate in our work. We own
a travel agency and have dedicated our lives to escort-
ing people on pilgrimages to the Holy Land. Together,
we are living and learning the life of Jesus, and trying
to follow in His footsteps. We are trying to be witnesses
to our faith by sharing our lives and our love with
others. In our own small way, we are contributing our
talents by reaching out and touching others who need
a visible sign of Christ in their lives. I am sure we are
not "there" yet by God's standards, but at least we are
on our way to becoming what God had in mind for us.

*Marie E. Ged is a homemaker who lives in Wayne,
N.J., and with her husband operates a travel agency.*

Experiencing the Lord

Joseph Mullen

My conversion continues to be slow and at times painful, especially when I don't trust. We recently moved from Greenwich, Connecticut, to San Francisco, leaving the community and parish of St. Catherine in Riverside—a community that had helped me grow from spiritual bankruptcy to knowing that I sin, but am forgiven.

My transfer to San Francisco was traumatic and left me wondering why, on those lonely weekends during the transition, away from my family, I experienced the Lord many times:

■ In a nun who one Sunday came up to me on the street, and said to me, "Smile, Jesus loves you!" She chatted for a while, and reminded me of what I had heard on my cursillo weekend—that Jesus is in me and loves me.

■ On my new job, with all the unknowns and the challenges, I found people crying out for help in handling themselves and their jobs. I would say often, "Why ask me?" Then I realized it was perhaps because I had a message to offer.

■ In a parish that had been the Council of Trent in the flesh, with no interest in reaching out or forming a community, which was depressing when compared with our Connecticut experience. Then on the very month we arrived there came a new pastor who began by saying, "I am here to serve you: help me!" He has since asked me to help start the cursillo movement: there is much to do.

■ In a wife and children whose lives my transfer has radically changed. Notwithstanding their separation from family and friends, they love me more than I thought possible. Christ was with us on Christmas day, our first away from the family, and yet the most peaceful.

■ But most of all, in my wife herself who gave up the most in our move: participation in a prayer group at St. Catherine's that sustained her; only six credits away from a Master's degree in counseling; an easy one-and-a-half-hour drive to her parent's and yet she ecouraged me and supported me as I would expect Jesus to do.

I have a feeling our seven years in St. Catherine's prepared us for today. While I still have need to grow and to allow myself to be loved, that will happen as we give to St. Monica's in Moraga, California.

I am aware of Christ's guidance and love more and more each day as I grudgingly give up control.

Joseph Mullen practices law in San Francisco.

Life, Hope and Love

Sister Mary Frances Hush, O.P.

For me, Jesus is life and hope, because He is love. And He reveals the Father's love.

I met Him through the eyes of my mother's faith. Her first child was retarded, and I was number two. Four others followed us. I was still young when I noticed Patty was different, but she was so much a part of our family and so loved I believed she would be like everyone else some day.

Awareness came gradually: No, Patty would always be different. Torturing questions began to haunt me: "Why was she like this? Didn't God love her as much as the rest of us?

"Why didn't He protect her from merciless teasing by neighborhood youngsters who could only see what was wrong?"

Always, mother had a patient, God-filled answer: "Yes, God does love Patty. He loves her so much that He can let her share some of His own suffering. The other children don't understand what they are doing: Jesus loves them too. Some day, they will see Patty as we do at home." Then I noticed how often mother would slip off to Mass in the morning. I began to want to know better this God who meant so much to her.

He was not long in teaching me He had a thousand

faces. I could find Him everywhere—in joy or sorrow, in "big" events and in ordinary ones, in family, friends, teachers, in the seas and the flowers, and even in the mighty thunderstorms. I was fascinated by them and never had enough sense to realize the danger of "walking through a storm."

God began to be so much a part of my life that I could not live without Him. Life was full of joy, excitement, dreams . . . But all paled next to this One Need. His call was insistent, yet gentle; persistent, but loving. It had to be all or nothing.

I knew I could find Him, or at least be best able to search for Him in the cloister. I was not wrong. He is ever the Faithful One, the Merciful Lover, the God who loves enough to ask for all, and then provides the strength to answer, "Yes!"

And now, He is the God-to-be-communicated, the God-to-be-lived-for-others, the God-TO-BE, and to be known at the very core of every person's being.

Sister Mary Frances Hush is a cloistered Dominican nun from the Monastery of the Blessed Sacrament in Farmington, Mich.

I Am Loved

Brother Robert Calabrese, O.F.M. Cap.

For me, Jesus the Christ is the first person I've ever risked falling in love with. I risked losing all security in my defenses, pains and passions, and most of all in my fears.

Jesus taught me how to receive love: to allow myself to be touched and affirmed by His gentle healing presence. And now that He has attained the depth of my spirit, I no longer hide from love, and no longer wonder, "Where could I go to escape from You? Where could I flee from Your presence?" For I know love, and I know trust, and I know they are meant to be shared.

Brother Robert Calabrese is a Franciscan studying for the priesthood at Immaculate Conception Seminary in Mahwah, N.J.

My Pilgrimage

Barbara Damato

About seven years ago, a dramatic change occurred in my life. I discovered the God of Love through His Son Jesus Christ. I realized that, with His unconditional love, I was a worthwhile person, both needed and accepted. I will try to share with you my pilgrimage from a life filled with self-doubt and fear to one filled with love, confidence, joy and self-attainment, through the discovery of the God of Love who makes every day of my life a beautiful day.

As a child, I had been taught to believe in a God of fear. A loving God was mentioned occasionally, but the God of fear took the spotlight. He kept a ledger-account of everything I did. Being human, I fell short of the expectations of this God, and was constantly plagued by a burden of fear and self-condemnation. Is it any wonder that my self-image was almost destroyed before it had a chance to grow?

In my 20s, I finally broke away from this God of fear who held me captive, and I started my search for a key to the meaning and purpose of my existence. Since I believed the Bible verse, "Seek and ye shall find," I was determined to find a better way to live. I read books on different religions, talked to informed people, took courses in consciousness-raising, and studied astrology.

After several years of praying and searching, I discovered the God of Love through His Son Jesus Christ. Because I had been blinded by my fears, I was unaware that He'd been there all the time.

The climax of this discovery came when I made a cursillo weekend. The cursillo is a three-day crash course in Christianity which allowed me to see what a true Christian community could be like. I was deeply moved by the love and open sharing that occurred on that weekend, and I wanted to remain a part of it. I decided then to follow the teachings of Jesus Christ. Peace and joy filled my heart and I felt cleansed in spirit. My life since then has never been the same.

One of the positive changes has been my attitude towards others. Before knowing Jesus, I judged everyone harshly as the God of fear judged me. Now, I accept people the way they are, and realize we all have to live in our own unique way. Some beautiful friendships have developed now that I am vulnerable and open with others. True friends need to be open and non-judgmental. Now I can be that kind of friend because I have inner security and confidence in myself.

Knowing Christ has helped me to make decisions without worry. I can face challenging situations with confidence. Without Christ, I never would have decided to earn a college degree. Trying to be a good wife and mother, keeping a large home clean, and earning a college degree in five years or less is not an easy task! I have a goal, and with Jesus' help, I will make it a reality.

I do not claim in any way to have all the answers, but I do know that following Christ is the way for me. Following Him has made my life a joy and a privilege, and has made the burdens lighter. I've had many painful decisions to make in the last seven years, and with His help, they've been good ones.

My life is now a positive one. While looking forward to the challenges on my pilgrimage, I try not to lose sight of the present day. I've learned to relax and take the time to enjoy the little gifts that make every day special: a child's hug or kiss, a beautiful flower, a "Hello" note from a distant friend. There's a little motto placed in a strategic spot in my home which says it all: "Live one day at a time—and make it a masterpiece!"

Barbara Damato is a homemaker in Wayne, N.J.

Growing Up

Murray Ballantyne

As a child, I saw every week on a glorious church window over the Communion table the words of St. Paul: "For me, to live is Christ and to die is gain." As I left the church with my parents and brothers, I faced another window proclaiming the words: "For I can do all things in him who strengtheneth me."

The long years since my childhood have been spent in beginning to realize the utter truth of these words. When I was young and strong, I admired the texts without taking them to heart. I had health and vigor, and was born to power and success: I felt sufficient.

When at the age of twenty-four I became a Catholic, I tried to put my talents and advantages at the service of the church. I was full of good ideas for the apostolate. Moreover, I thought people could be argued into faith—so I worked for the Catholic press, and for bookshops, labor schools and the like. It took me a long and painful time to realize I was making two great errors: I tended to tell God what to do instead of asking Him what, if anything, He wanted me to do. The second error was trying to do things *for* people instead of *with* them. Everything I touched eventually failed.

At one time, I reveled in doctrine and felt sure of

many things. Then, somehow, words ceased to be wholly satisfying. Theology is talking about God, but it is not God. I began to face Him, the ineffable, in the darkness of my soul.

Slowly, it became clear that all my talents, my advantages, my "strengths" were not really mine at all: they were no more than loans. The God who had given could take away. If God could raise up sons of Abraham out of these very stones, how could He be said to "need" me? I looked within and found I was nothing.

Yet, there is a sense in which God can be said to "need" us. Because He made us free, He cannot enter our hearts unless we hold them open; He cannot enter our souls except to the extent in which we make room for Him. There is after all one thing we can offer Him, and that is our *fiat,* our acceptance. We need to empty ourselves in order to be filled. As we learn to rely less on ourselves, we come to rely more and more on Him. We are called to become engrafted into Christ. In Him we live and move and have our being.

When we find this path (or almost absence of path), our trials and sufferings will not be less. They may well be more. But now Christ will be not only with us but also in us. In Him we can find the strength to endure. God did not become man to end suffering, but to share it. The deeper my suffering, the greater the darkness, the more do I hold His hand.

Now truly we find that we can do all things and endure all things in Him who strengtheneth us. Let us walk humbly so that the day may come when we too may say with St. Paul, "For me, to live is Christ and to die is gain."

I diminish, that He may increase.

Jesus, my Brother, my Life, my Hope!

Murray Ballantyne is retired and lives in Montreal, Que., Canada.

The Experience of Faith in Christ

Msgr. Peter J. Hill

The best way for me to describe and to sense Christ's presence in my life is by seeing how I've lived with Him. Looking back can give a deep appreciation of God's workings in one's life, an awareness of many things unnoticed while they were happening, but significant when remembered.

The first phase of my contact with Jesus was, naturally, the Christian way of life I received from my family, through their example and traditions. My parents were Catholics in the Netherlands—where Catholics have been persecuted for three hundred years. When my parents were still young, things began to get better, but the country's tradition remained Calvinistic. My mother used to tell us "Don't make trouble where trouble can be avoided; stick to essentials, and never mind the frills and the trimmings."

Our devotions were never excessive. We didn't talk much about religion—but there was an inner *feeling* about it: this was the way we should be directed in all things. Every evening, my mother would lead the family and guests in prayer. Morning prayers were private. Prayer was used to provide a moment of rest in God's presence.

When I was thirteen, I decided to enter the seminary.

After six years of traditional, solid training, I went on to specialized studies in Louvain University. As I look back on these early years, I realize that the religious experience was something external, something I accepted as long as it didn't take over my whole self. I was holding back.

In the Old Testament, the Jewish people tried to satisfy God with sacrifices. I seemed to be doing the same, although the prophets tried to convince the Israelites that God wanted the conversion of hearts.

After I became a missionary in Santa Fé, New Mexico, I found out that although I was willing to work for others, I had not yet surrendered my whole life. Little by little, as I tried to remain faithful to my vocation— through meditation, and prayer, and offerings—it finally dawned on me that there was more of myself to be given in order to make my efforts fruitful. But first, reverses, personality clashes, misunderstandings, disappointments and illness had to start a cleansing process. All this, expressed in one short sentence, took many years.

During the thirty years I was teaching in the seminary, contact with sick people and weekend parish work began to make me see how difficulties can bring one closer to emptying oneself, so that God can take over. It is then that, as St. Paul says, you are one body and one spirit with Christ, or at least hope to become one with him. The experience of faith in Christ, of contact with Him through people, makes everything else unimportant. As St. Paul, again, puts it: "I have pitched out all the rest." Only whatever is in unity with this one body and one spirit can be for the good of God's kingdom.

Besides contact with Jesus through people, there is also the essential communication with Him through the Eucharist. To me, the Real Presence is a fact beyond apologetics. I agree with a little verse attributed to Queen Elizabeth the First:

> *His was the Word that spake it.*
> *He took the bread and brake it.*
> *And what the Word doth make it,*
> *So I believe—and take it.*

Whatever it is, that's what it *is!* Let it go at that. It will always remain a mystery, an experience of faith.

St. John writes that no one has seen God, but that we have seen Christ. When I experience Him, I can experience God, because He is both man and God. I can talk to Him readily, because He is a man like me—but He also expands me, because He is God.

Msgr. Hill, a retired missionary priest, formerly taught at Immaculate Heart of Mary Seminary in Santa Fe, N.M.

Images of Jesus

Father Simon Reynolds, O.C.S.O.

The question is, "For you, who is Jesus Christ?" St. Thomas Aquinas could not answer competently, even in his monumental *Summa*. So after I am finished, be assured there is much more to be said about Jesus who is my Lord, my God, my All.

In my cell, above my all-purpose table (I have no desk), I have tacked three "miraculous" pictures. One is of the Shroud of Turin. It images God the Father. How do I know? Jesus said, "He who sees Me sees the Father." It is a clear image of the First Person, because the Passion had destroyed all other items that added up to Jesus. It has the majesty of the Ancient of the Days, not the benign countenance of a young man of thirty-three years.

A "live" shot of Jesus is next to our Father. A charitable parishioner donates a tabernacle for his church's main altar. He takes a photo of it for his records. The developed picture shows the most beautiful Jesus face I ever could imagine. The eyes are marvelous, penetrating, divine. And the tabernacle? There is no trace whatsoever in the developed film of the object the camera was aimed at!

The third out-of-this world picture is that of Our Lady of Guadalupe. The artist: Mary herself. She painted it on a Mexican peasant's scapular to convince a doubting archbishop that she wanted a chapel where her basilica now dominates Mexico City. When I look at her, I see Jesus, for He and she for nine months were physically one: she the tabernacle, He the indwelling God, photographed by my mental film-picture when my mind would have her for its object.

For me too, Jesus Christ is the consecrated bread, the consecrated wine. At Mass, after consecration, the film of my soul registers the face of Jesus, where before there had been nothing but bread on the paten and wine in the chalice.

Father Simon is a Trappist monk of Our Lady of Guadalupe Abbey in Lafayette, Ore.

Following Him

Mary Sullivan

Who is Jesus to me? I find it difficult to separate Him from the Trinity. It has taken a lifetime to merge Father, Son and Spirit—and the mystery remains.

I am told, and I hear Him say (in the Scriptures) that He is the Way. I do not contradict that, but I am at a loss to describe how Jesus fuses with Father and Spirit to be One who has dominion over me and all creation. That I alternate between being daughter, sister, friend and spouse is a fact: how it came to *be* is known only to Him! Perhaps I said "yes" and really meant it once—and He took me at my word!

I have traveled a long road, following Him. I have listened and tried to do so when He placed me behind His right shoulder with the admonition to "see people as He sees them"; have identified with the Canaanite woman (flat on her face, begging for another's release from evil); have assumed the *adsum* position: here am I, Lord: do with me what you will; have danced before Him in excess of joy at the thought of being His; have begged leave to withdraw from His presence (fear and awe!); have counted the world and all in it well lost for His sake—impedimenta on the journey to Him; have had the certainty that it was enough to put myself in His presence (weak, confused, sinful, but graced!); have endured the pain of His loving gaze; have experienced the incomprehensible joy (and rejoiced in it!) that flows from the wound in Jesus' side (the final wound that released the Father's forgiveness) and identified with both the Crucified and the crucifiers . . . for I am both.

And have arrived *where?* And who is *He* to *me?* I am, I see, in Merton's palace of Nowhere—at last! I am *nothing*—and *everything*—since *He* would have it so. And *He* is like a lover for whom I yearn: I seek (as in the Song of Songs) but do not find. I live in "bright darkness," trusting Him whom I have so painfully learned to trust.

I have learned to let go in every area of my mortal life: of friends who are the other halves of my soul, of my children, of ambition, and power, and control: all gone! And in the moments when whatever wisdom I have learned comes into play, and I let go of *Him* whom my soul seeks, He comes with glad surprise to fill me and transport me.

Less of me brings more of Him!

Mary Sullivan, a writer, lives in Holyoke, Mass.

Peace Beyond Understanding

José de Vinck

For me, before all else, Jesus is "peace beyond understanding."

Particularly after Communion, there comes from the bottom of my being a deep spiritual sigh, a releasing of the steam of all anguish, a throwing overboard of any kind of worry, present and future, about my own fate, that of my family, and that of the world: an inexplicably profound feeling that in spite of the pain of living, in spite of the horror and malice so visible around us, "all manner of things shall be well," as Dame Julian of Norwich said so beautifully.

There is another aspect of the reality of Christ which strikes me powerfully and is not sufficiently expressed in the church ritual of the Mass: His actual presence among us, now, "wherever two or three are gathered in His name," or wherever even one is seeking Him in solitude.

There is something sadly lacking in the official formula, "Christ has died, Christ is risen, Christ will come again." I would greatly rejoice on the day when a better sense of theology would have all Christians proclaim together: "Christ has died, Christ is risen, *Christ is with us,* Christ will come again *in glory.*"

José de Vinck, a publisher and author, lives in Allendale, N.J.

Christ in People

Maureen Cannon

For me, Jesus Christ is not only my closest and most intimate friend, but He is manifested almost daily, forcefully (and beautifully) in the people with whom I come in contact. "Ordinary" days are made extraordinary by chance encounters, by human intercourse that moves the heart or lifts the spirit or is shaped like laughter. I call these "blessings," and I thank Jesus Christ for them.

He works through people in the dark days too. When my beloved husband died two years ago, during those black and terrifying weeks of his dying, and through the long, uphill journey since, there was Jesus Christ beside me. But oh, also, there were the friends.

Some had been friends since childhood. Our friendships had weathered storms for more than fifty years. This was the biggest, the most pain-filled storm. It was my holocaust. They were there, the dear old friends, reaching out to comfort and sustain, each one granting me what seemed to me his or her own particular radiance, bearing witness to the incredible depths of the human spirit. Who gave each one of them such extraordinary empathy at so sorrowful a time? Who discovered my need even while I was trying to hide it? Who taught them how to provide the most effective help? I think the answer is: Jesus Christ.

There were strangers, too, two years ago. In a city as vast and impersonal as New York, strangers paused in their busy pursuits to—suddenly, somehow, and to my grateful amazement—make me feel very much a part of the human family.

I was racing from the hospital one frightening night (racing from a room and a nightmare and a future I didn't think I could possibly face) when a bus-driver, in mid-block, not only stopped his crowded bus to pick me up (I had missed it at the corner), but even came down the steps to help me. Why? How did he know how desperately I needed that particular kindness at that hour? Wait, let me not ask "Why," but "Who?" I answer: Jesus Christ.

It was Jesus, too, who spoke through the little man on the same hospital corner when, embarrassed to discover I had no change to pay for the soda I'd ordered and opened, I was told not to worry. "You can pay me any time," said the vendor. Gently! This kind of trust in New York City? Of course—if Jesus is there.

These may seem like small incidents: they were life-giving to me.

And Jesus is there, He is here, always. He gave me then, and He gives me still, not only Himself, but Himself-in-others, friends for the black times and the happy ones, and strangers also for both. They are His gifts, and they are what He means to me.

Maureen Cannon, a poet and librarian, lives in Ridgewood, N.J.

A Journey With a Friend

Father Richard Liddy

In 1965, I was a young priest doing graduate studies
in philosophy in Rome. The Second Vatican Council
had been going on for several years and the first rum-
blings of *aggiornamento* were beginning to be heard
throughout the church. Some friends had already begun
to leave the priesthood—including some very gifted
priests who were also graduate students.

One night in the spring I went out for a walk in
Rome with a priest a few years older than myself. He
had spent a year with the Trappists and was now pre-
paring to teach Scripture in a large mid-western diocese.
Rome, in those days, was a delightful place to stroll in
the evening, and converse about everything and anything.

At the Piazza Argentino, we stopped for a pizza in
a little pizzeria located on the second floor of a building next to the old Teatro. As we conversed, I waxed
eloquent on what was wrong with the church, and particularly what was wrong with the hierarchy. A talented
and gifted friend had just left the priesthood to get married, and I was saying in effect, "If only those people
would get beyond this legalism of celibacy, we would
not be losing all those talented people." As I spoke, I
became more vehement in pointing the finger where

I thought blame for the situation resided—primarily in "them."

My friend listened patiently, and then said something that literally perplexed me: "I need to be saved; I need someone who knows what it means to be human. . . . But I need more: I need Jesus."

My heart and mind stopped. I was hurt, and hurt deeply. "Why did he have to say that?" I asked myself. "I took *that* for granted. Why bring in religion when I'm talking about church politics?"

I think I argued with him a bit—I don't quite remember. But I do remember that as we walked home that evening through the streets of Rome, I felt the hurt deep in my heart. It took me at least a week to come to terms with that wound—and I'm still trying to come to terms with it.

The major part of that "coming to terms" has been a deeper commitment to prayer. I had assumed my religious life; I had become a priest; I celebrated the liturgy and prayed periodically; I claimed that praying was what was important, not "getting into" the Breviary. But my life didn't represent a vital bridging between my heart and my "opinions." What came from me were mental-trips reflecting my anger and prejudices —not the Gospel forming in my heart and mind so as to make me live in the real church, in the real world.

Some time later, my friend gave me a small leather-bound edition of the Scriptures and encouraged me to pray with it frequently. After listening to him and even sharing my own heart and hurts with him, he pointed me, not primarily to his judgments—which have been very sound through the years—but to the Word of God.

"Take just a couple of lines of the Gospels," he said, "and imagine the scene: Jesus, the Apostles, the countryside, the lake; and hear Jesus speaking His Word to you, very uniquely and personally."

Years later, I found out such an approach was of the essence of Ignatian contemplation. The renewal in our own time of this and other types of prayer convinces me that many people need and are searching for a deeper experiential knowledge of Jesus.

We're on a journey with a Friend. This is a great and beautiful mystery to be lived, not a problem to be solved.

Father Liddy, a priest of the Newark, N.J., Archdiocese, teaches at the North American College in Rome.

Friendship and Christ

Father Guy Tillson, O.F.M. Cap.

Some years ago, the relationship I had with a very trusted and beloved friend went through a period of severe turbulence. The cause of most of the difficulty was my own insecurity, possessiveness and jealousy. It reached such a level of rage and fury that the two of us barely spoke to each other. The discord was most grievous to me, so I thought to let the friendship go rather than continue hurting the both of us by my childish behavior.

I was very active in the charismatic renewal at the time. A few days after my decision to surrender this relationship, our prayer group had its weekly meeting. That night, one of the leaders took us through a prayer for healing in which we had to use our imagination.

The prayer-image she constructed was taken from John's Gospel, the thirteenth chapter—Jesus washing the feet of His disciples. As she embellished the story, and as I beheld it in the deep recesses of my heart's eye, the face of Christ was the face of my friend! It was a very uncomfortable prayer, and I must have balked and resisted as much as Peter did! But one phrase kept turning over in my mind—Jesus' words, "If I do not wash you, you cannot be my disciple."

Throughout the next week, these words recurred

constantly. Though the situation between my friend and myself did not improve, I began to realize that my surrender had to be done in love and not in resentment. As painful as it was, I had to allow the vision of Christ with my friend's face to truly cleanse me. Jesus had to perform that service for me, if I was to understand truly what His own humility meant.

I wept. I groaned. I felt more lonely and unloved than I ever had before. Yet by the week's end there came the awareness that my dearest friend was Jesus Himself.

At the next week's prayer meeting another woman got up at one point and spoke briefly about her own relationship with Jesus. She concluded by saying, "He is my greatest friend." I felt a true recognition of my own love for Jesus at that moment, and that relationship has grown and deepened in the time that has passed since then.

Though I still deeply value the intimacy of human friendship, the love my heart needs is always filled by the Lord Himself. He is my closest companion, my most faithful friend, and I would go so far as to say he is my most gentle and compassionate lover.

Father Tillson, a Franciscan, is a member of the faculty at Don Bosco College, Newton, N.J.

Jesus Means Freedom

Marie Poulin

I was brought up in a family where religion played an important role: from beliefs to practices to moral aspects of behavior. In early adulthood, my idealistic views on love, marriage, manhood were smashed, along with my ego, my hopes, my love of life: a divorce. I became angry, at myself, at Jesus Christ. I could not understand: why?

Nearly ten years have passed. What happened during those ten years that transformed my anger into peace of heart? Why do I say today, "Thank you, Lord, for past and future experiences"?

I slowly became aware of my emotional and spiritual immaturity. In my free time, I took courses: transcendental meditation, yoga, etc. I learned a lot, but remained "hungry." Through my relationship with friends, through their generosity, their understanding, something struck home: I understood I was bitter; and I lived a new experience, *grace,* a true gift of God to mankind.

You see, I found out that I could not forgive on my own: my hurt was too deep. I began reading the New Testament. Through the words, through Jesus Christ's life, I wondered: "If God gave His only Son to the world, for the redemption of mankind, how much He must love us."

I asked God, "Teach me to forgive, as You forgive." I asked not once, not twice, but during months, years. Our time is not God's time. Looking back, I now realize His time was the best time, because He took my hand and said, "Hang in there, and you will grow."

The growing was a daily process and still is. The daily exercise: the New Testament. We have been taught that God is a judge. I have learned that if we realized for a single moment the extent of His love, we would be so overwhelmed that our desire for eternal life (death) would be immediate.

Through His Son, I am learning patience; and through the Holy Spirit, I am discovering that He spreads His gifts among people, so that we may form together a true "community," more complete in this union than we would be on our own.

Jesus Christ means freedom: forgiveness for the past, responsibility for our choices, less worry for the future. Since our choices range from daily attitudes and relationships to distant goals and the establishment of a style of life, I need His wisdom, patience, light.

Marie Poulin is director of the Canadian Broadcasting Company (Radio Canada) in Sudbury, Ont., Canada, where she lives.

The Lord of the Dance

Carla De Sola

The vocation God has given me is to dance and pray. The meaning of Jesus, who He is, the epiphany of His presence, seems clearest to me when I am practicing this ministry.

Dancing, without separation from prayer, is sometimes a conscious communion with the Lord as a living center in my heart, radiating outward.

In workshops, I teach a simple exercise that expresses this thought. It begins with the hands curved inwards toward the heart, torso bent forward, and then reaching outward in a flowing motion coordinated with the breath while the torso unfolds.

One would think that with the motion of dancing, it might be hard to keep to a still center—yet the opposite is true when a center is found which generates the flow of movement. Then there's an at-one-ment of spirit and body, a sense of wholeness. It is in this experience that I perceive the uplifting power of the spirit; it is while dancing that I take the chance that God is there.

Most of the time when I am just *being* (moving, living, dancing,) I take for granted a hidden presence of God. The way I perceive this unseen involvement of God in daily life is, of course, affected by my training as a dancer. When practicing and performing, there is no time to think of all the hidden muscles and nerve coordination responsible for the movements of my body: hundreds of signals are needed just to lift a finger. To stop and think so minutely, even if it were possible, would result in cutting the flow of unity between movement and muscle, between myself and the dance. Why stop the flow of the soul's communion with God in daily life?

When I stop and "think," looking for the presence of Jesus so as to know who He is, He disappears. Then I am led to "seek Him whom my soul loves."

I seek Him by communing, as if I were in the silence of the desert. At such times, my awareness of life's pervasiveness, with its sounds and motions, within and without, is reawakened and centers me in the Lord.

The Communion most precious to me occurs during or after dancing at a liturgy. My heart is then awakened by the love of Jesus, and I become deeply united with the congregation. The presence of the Lord seems to fill the place of worship.

During a recent charismatic conference, while dancing under the night sky after rain, this gloriously occurred on the ball field of Yankee Stadium! I saw Jesus as Lord both of the day and of the night.

Carla De Sola is director of the Omega Liturgical Dance Company, which is in residence at the Cathedral of St. John the Divine in New York.

"A Waiting With Certitude"

Father John Catoir

My love and understanding of Jesus have deepened over the years. As a boy in a Catholic grammar school, I learned He was a Divine Person. I'm not sure what that meant to me at the time: I don't remember being especially pious. But I was an altar boy, and I loved to serve Mass—especially funerals because they got us out of class.

During college, I began taking Jesus more seriously. His attraction disturbed me: I wanted to be free, unfettered by religious scruples. Jesus quickly drew me closer. I became dimly aware that He was asking something of me, perhaps the priesthood. But no, that would be too much, I reasoned. I'll give my life to God, but on my own terms.

That defense only extended the agony of my resistance. For six years, I managed to deny the desire growing within me, more out of fear of failing than anything else. It was while I was in the Army, a draftee after graduating from college, that I yielded my life to Christ. In the very act of surrendering to Him, I discovered that I truly wanted to be a priest. In spite of my insecurity, I knew that trust in His strength was the only weapon I needed.

As I write this, I am approaching my 21st anniversary as a priest of Jesus Christ.

What does Jesus mean to me? Much more than I can say. What does water mean to a fish, or air to a bird? Paul put it so well: "In him I live and breathe and have my being."

The joys of the priesthood have far exceeded my wildest expectations; the burdens, though heavy at times, were nothing compared with those of Christ. My greatest difficulty came when I tried to do too much on my own. I learned the painful lesson that without Him I am nothing, and my life is meaningless; but with Him, in Him, through Him I am becoming a new creation.

I love Jesus. He has given me both happiness and hope. Dante described hope as "a waiting with certitude."

Father Catoir, a priest of the Paterson, N.J., Diocese, is the director of The Christophers and the author of "Enjoy the Lord" and other books.

Jesus Is the Answer

Beryl Orris

Experience in education has taught me that I cannot teach anyone unless he has the desire to learn. Even if the individual wants to learn, however, I cannot teach him anything outside his own frame of reference.

It was impossible for mankind to grasp the infinite concept that God is Love. Therefore it became necessary that Love be placed into man's frame of reference in order for Him to be understood. So the Word was made flesh: Love became incarnate in Jesus Christ so that through His life, precept and example, mankind became capable of understanding.

In Jesus' life and personality, I am able to understand an infinite principle because it has been translated into my finite context.

Because Jesus took unto himself total humanity, He is then able to say to me, "These things I do, you too will do." Now I begin to see that my prime vocation is not the priesthood, religious life, or anything else. That may come later. My primary vocation is the call to become a human being.

Because Jesus Christ has come into my world, He has set forth the blueprint of my life, he has given me to understand who I have been called to become. He has also assured me that it is possible for me to answer that call.

This is what Jesus Christ means to me. When people ask me, "What is a human being? Who is the one after whom you should pattern yourself to become whom you are called to be?" Jesus is the answer—yesterday, today and always.

Beryl Orris, a psychologist, was one of Freud's last students and now lives in London, Ont., Canada.

The Presence of Christ

Rev. Nan Hirleman

I spent one of my college years in England, and it was during those months that I experienced a sense of emptiness difficult to describe. At times, it expressed itself through anxious tears; at other times, through a pervasive emotional numbness. Perhaps emptiness is not the right word. Maybe these times I'm speaking of were actually a kind of fullness, being full of the fear that perhaps there really was no reason to start another day.

Somehow, I connect that growing numbness with our tours of the Roman ruins of northern England. Stones of other worlds were barely visible amidst small tufts of grass. People had lived there. They had dreamed dreams, raised children and stirred warm brews in heavy pots. That their dwellings were now in ruins, and the object of our detached speculation, planted the seeds of despair in me.

My images of these ruins shaped themselves into a haunting question: can life matter at all if it ends in ruins? The rooms I lived in, the friendships I began, the tasks of each day, seemed meaningless in the face of their eventual end.

As I look back on those months in England, it seems as though the deepest and most sensitive part of my being was seeing human life raw and unfiltered by simple answers. That wisest part of me—my soul—was longing for a word or touch that would give me a reason to begin the day.

It was in late winter of that year that I was faced by familiar, frightening and hopeful words: "Either you are for Me or against Me." The choice seemed stark and unshaded by possible interpretations.

I came to see the "Me" of that statement as the deepest and ultimate Presence in the universe . . . and my soul's dearest friend. I came to believe it was a friendship that was no substitute for love of family and friends, but rather one that gathers up, holds and fulfills my other relationships. I came to see that choosing to accept the love and friendship of Christ was to become awake to all the beauty, tenderness, suffering, challenge and hope that are present in the very texture of the universe.

There was a poignant and almost heartbreaking fullness in the air that spring. The flowers I saw early in the morning hinted to me of the unutterable beauty of God's imagination. One afternoon, walking behind a lumbering old woman, I was filled with love for her as for someone with whom I was connected, as the branches are connected to the vine. I felt as though I were seeing Reality for the first time—seeing that life *is* precious and meaningful, even if it changes or ends, because we are living in the very presence of a God who never dies, a God who continually seeks us and offers us His love.

In those months of spring, I could sense the nearness of Christ. I was aware that Christ *is* alive—that Christ

is risen to be with us. I came to see Christ seeking each
one of us, reaching out to where each one of us most
needs to be met, Christ touching our souls and offering
Himself to us that we may live.

*The Reverend Nan Hirleman is associate pastor of
St. Francis Lutheran Church in San Francisco.*

Christ Fully Human

Frederick Franck, M.D.

The meaning of Jesus in my life? This meaning is that He is the Christ, the very epitome of the meaning of human life and its Pioneer. To quote my translation of Angelus Silesius:

> If Christ were born a million times in Galilee,
> He lived, nor died, nor rose
> unless He is awakened in me.

The Christ-nature is the core of our being, the indestructible, specifically human element at our center, the Unborn, the indwelling Spirit. Once we are awakened, the Christ-nature becomes Christ-consciousness, not before. Once we are awakened, we participate, "communicate" in the crucifixion of the ego-delusion, and hence in the resurrection of the truly human.

Jesus cries out, "Why have you forsaken Me?" and, "In your hands I commend My spirit." These are supreme signs of humanness. Since Christ is the lodestar and image of the fully human, He calls upon us to contemplate ourselves in this mirror, and to know the mystery of our existence and be liberated by the truth of human reality.

When He says, "Follow Me," He bids us, not to

imitation, but to the following of the Christ-nature that is the Truth at our core. But what is this but words? ... Who has ever formulated it adequately, except St. John in the first chapter of his Gospel. I can only mumble. . . .

Frederick Franck is an author, an internationally known artist and a dental surgeon who now lives in Warwick, N.Y. One of his books, "Days With Albert Schweitzer," is an account of his service at the Albert Schweitzer Hospital in Africa.

"For You, Darkness Itself Is Not Dark" (Psalm 139)

K. R.

Only when I know I am loved do I know most truly who I am created to be, and this is most clear in my experience before the Lord Jesus.

In moments of grace which reveal His presence, I *know* without hesitation He is the air I breathe—and it is good. I *know* He sees me through and through—and that, too, is good. I *know* He sees my limits and fears, my sins and blindness. He does not overlook them as though they did not matter to Him, or were somehow outside His caring: He restores all to wholeness by His mercy.

Some years ago, I was suffering from a terrible depression, unable to break free from the pull towards death and destruction. One night was particularly filled with agitation; exhaustion and anxiety engulfed me, and suddenly for a single moment I became clearly aware of the presence of Jesus, of Light. And in that moment, I knew He was faithful to me, my constant companion. I knew I was loved. This experience broke through my feelings of abandonment, and for the first time in months, I slept peacefully.

The light receded. I was not cured overnight; months of pain, therapy and struggle lay ahead. Yet somehow a seed of hope had been planted, though I dared not

look at it for fear that it, too, like everything else that
had been good, would disappear. But it survived there
in the darkness and took root. As I look back, it seems
to me as if I had been holding within me a secret frag-
ment of life that remained secret even to me—for I
dared not claim it; I thought it too fragile. Unable to
withstand the darkness at a time when I knew only
darkness.

> *Such things are too wonderful for me,*
> *too marvelous for me to behold.*
> *I am fearfully, wonderfully made. . . .*
> *Wonderful are your works. (Ps. 139)*

Jesus continues to heal me, to bind up my wounds
of shame—shame of things I cannot name, shame of
failures quite nameable, shame of being ashamed. This
shame distorts, disfigures. And the healing oil which
transforms me and makes me whole is the beauty and
light of Christ Jesus the Lord, revealing Himself in
me, in others, in all His words. His beauty teaches me
who I am, tells me that I am loved. "For your darkness
shines in the day." (Ps. 139)

K.R. lives and work in Regina, Sask., Canada.

The Jewish Cosmic King

Richard Simon Hanson, Ph.D.

Jesus Christ is the Jew in my life. As He meets me
in the pages of the New Testament He is for ever and
ever the Jew. Whether in Matthew, where His Jewish
vocabulary is strong, or in the universal projections of
John, this Nazarene of the Gospels is a flower that
blooms on a Jewish stem. To accept this one as Lord
is to accept all Jews as brothers and sisters. He is a
character in Jewish history, and the Jew in our history.

Jesus as seed cast into the ground arose to become
the beginning of a body seen by the Apostle Paul as
the Cosmic Christ, the Jewish Messiah become Hope
of the World. All who heed the cry of the messenger
who proclaims that Hope become members of that
Body as it emerges from the womb of the earth in
travail. I am part of that Body.

Jesus the King to be served and honored by my work
and my adoration is that Jesus who meets me in the
eyes of my neighbor in need, in the hunger and thirst,
the pain and loneliness of those who live about me in
my own time. He comes to me in the guise of you my
companion, and you the stranger. He comes with dirty
feet I am compelled to wash. That act declares your

worth as my Lord in disguise, and my worth as His
servant.

*Prof. Hanson holds his doctorate from Harvard Uni-
versity and is an author and professor of religion at
Luther College in Decorah, Iowa.*

From Alienation to Belonging

Romeo Maione

During my Catholic school years, the church had not been able to give my life a meaning—nor had the surrounding culture of the time. The industrial world of today has made of man an object. "You are a number." "You can be replaced." "Remember you are nothing."

The little cell of a world where parents gave proof that you were important, not on account of what you produced, but on account of what you were, their son, seemed then so far away. Entering a modern factory is like plunging into an alienating world where a man becomes less than nothing. The church is not aware of such a world. My family did not know about such dehumanizing an atmosphere. The church was unable to speak the language of this new industrial milieu. My family was still speaking the language of the village.

I gave up on the church; I gave up on the family; I became alienated.

Then one day a priest talked to me about life, my life. He cared for this wretched life of mine to the point of spending much time with me. The "I" which for me had lost all importance seemed for him to have absolute value.

This act of faith in me, coming from another, triggered an act of faith in myself. He introduced me to life, so that I could pass from there into his faith. He allowed me to enter into the company of his friend Jesus. I became someone who could believe and who had a future.

Can there be anything more tremendous than suddenly ceasing to be nothing and becoming someone, passing from alienation to the sonship of God?

An alienated being changes into a son, and in turn becomes an apostle of the truth. My gratitude to the church forces me to repeat the Apostles' question: "Lord, who else could we go to?"

Why do I remain in the church? The church has given me an opportunity to discover the Gospel; it has provided the strength I need to live the ideal of Christ; it has made me realize there will always be a creative minority promoting the Good News throughout the ages; and it has taught me that we are all weak and small men before the task entrusted to us: to "complete God's creation."

Romeo Maione of Ottawa is the former president of the International Young Christian Workers and is now with the Canadian International Development Agency.

The Lord Is My Life

Father Emeric A. Lawrence, O.S.B.

Judging by the Gospels, the question, "For you, who is Jesus?" is one that Jesus Himself wants each one of His followers to answer personally.

I am afraid that for several decades of my life, Jesus was pretty much a figure from the past—a very real historical figure, to be sure, but He was not present to me in the same way that a friend or a dear confrère might be present. I just didn't "experience" His presence.

Conditions began to improve in the late forties and early fifties, primarily through my contact with the writings of Cardinal Suhard (*The Meaning of God*) and of Father Louis Bouyer. Suhard presented a God who was simultaneously *transcendent* (the all-perfect, infinitely holy Being) and *immanent* (Emmanuel, God-with-us).

In *The Meaning of Monastic Life,* Bouyer wrote: "If it is truly God whom we seek, we have to seek Him as a person. . . . It is only in the 'I-Thou' relationship that the person remains personal for us." He also said that our whole concept of God changes when we begin to think of Him in terms of the second person (you) instead of the third (he). These ideas bolstered an "inspiration" I had already begun to put into practice

when I wrote *Meditating the Gospels* (1956); a book
in which I tried to speak directly to the Jesus presented
to us in the Sunday and feastday Gospels, asking Him
questions, and, I believe, receiving some pretty good
answers.

About this time, too, I read one of Dorothy Day's
columns in which she strongly recommended the "Jesus
prayer," and this prayer began to exercise a consider-
able influence on my prayer life. You cannot breathe
in and out or repeat again and again the phrase, "Lord
Jesus Christ, have mercy on me" without growing in
intimacy with Jesus, without His becoming more and
more vividly present to you.

So, as I look back to the past and try to follow the
unfolding of my friendship with Jesus, I have to con-
fess that arriving at a clear sense of Jesus' actual presence to and with me has been a gradual process—one
that I am not quite satisfied with. But can anyone ever
be completely satisfied in such matters as these? I am
not one who underwent a sudden, instantaneous conversion, as seems to be the case with many modern
Christians; my experience of Jesus has never been vivid
or sensational. But there is one thing I do know by
now: Jesus is real to me, as He never had been when
I was younger.

So if I am pinned down, my answer to the question,
"For you, who is Jesus Christ?" would be (and here I
am going to change to the second person): "You are
the Christ, the Son of the Living God. You are Lord,
the Lord of my life. But You are also Jesus my Brother,
You are the be-all and the end-all of my life. You are,
in the words of that good Frenchman François Mauriac,

'The One I love most in the world—and for this reason,
You are the One I have most betrayed'."

This might give the impression I am or have been
a sensational sinner, and I don't think it is true: just an
ordinary and commonplace sinner. I would like to add
something like this: if that last phrase sounds ex-
travagant, let us understand that in the context of the
love we owe Jesus, all or any sin is a betrayal.

*Father Lawrence, a Scripture scholar and writer
whose books include "The Week With Christ" and
"Becoming a Mature Christian," is chaplain and professor at St. Scholastica Priory and College in Duluth,
Minn.*

Starting Anew

Dolores Lynn de Vinck

Some years ago, I could not have answered the question, "Who is Jesus Christ in your life?" After growing up in an Irish Catholic home and being educated in Catholic schools, I could quote Scripture by heart and recite every rule the church had chosen to institute— and a few others besides. I never thought of Christ as a separate entity within the elusive being called God. This God was a judge before all else, whose purpose was to keep tabs on me.

My interpretation of religion was narrow and egotistical, so that it had become an imposition on my life. Going to Mass served only to spare me from eternal damnation. I got nothing in return, except the superficial fulfillment of an obligation. All I wanted was to be left in peace. I was willing to lead a good life on my own. I wasn't looking for license to sin, but I resented my conscience and all the guilt that went with it.

I never attained my childish wish of being able to drop formal religion, although I tried. I did the basic minimum required by "law" to alleviate guilt. I went to Mass on Sundays, usually late, and didn't bother about the Eucharist, because worry over my own worthiness made it too difficult. As long as I did not receive Communion, I did not have to face the feeling I had committed a sacrilege.

Confession consisted in rattling off a shopping list of offenses, as fast as possible, and like a real trip to the supermarket, it was the same items time after time. I never gave myself a chance to grow. I never talked to God, never listened, never once contemplated His love. It was a great waste of irreplaceable time, but since I never consciously chose to refuse any deeper relationship, I hope God will work this arid past to some good effect.

Growth, especially when it involves a positive change, is a slow, painful and continuing process. I am not aware of what changed in my life. I only know I reached a point where I could no longer cope with my kind of God. I was twenty, married, living in Canada. And I was a two-year-old in terms of religious development.

One night, we went to dinner at a neighbor's house. There was a huge poster in the kitchen: "GOD IS LOVE!" A very common item today, but it was the first time I had ever seen it. This inert piece of paper was my bolt of lightning. What a beautiful thought!

Then other things began to happen. I met a priest who was filled with the joy of Christ and his religion. He became a close friend and the godfather of my second son. I also became involved with a parish blessed with the leadership of an elderly but modern-thinking pastor. I no longer had to cringe and read the bulletin during hell-and-damnation sermons, because there were none. Positive, affirmative thoughts were offered instead.

I also had the opportunity to make many trips to
Madonna House, the lay apostolate center in Combermere, Ontario. There I came across happy, rejoicing
people. The germ of an idea had taken root: God
couldn't be as demanding and judgmental as I had
imagined, otherwise how could these people have become so deeply and freely involved with Him?

I had a strong desire to begin my religious education
all over again. I read, talked, listened and observed. I
absorbed everything like a dry sponge. I began to hear
a lot about Jesus and His love for mankind. He had
meaning for those around me, and they were strangely
joyous about it. For the first time, He began to have
meaning in my own life.

Now, answering the question as to who Jesus is in
my life, I would simply say: He IS. He is a loving
presence. I am only now beginning to learn.

*Dolores Lynn de Vinck is a mother and high school
teacher and lives in Ramsey, N.J.*

Jesus Is Mercy

Father Ignatius Kacumanu

"Father, forgive them, for they do not know what they are doing."

"But I say to you, love your enemies and pray for those who hate you, pray for those who treat you with contempt, and to him who strikes you on one cheek, offer the other also. . . ."

Mahatma Gandhi was moved to the very core of his being when he read for the first time these mysterious words from the New Testament. In fact, these words were the actual basis for his famous weapon of Satyagraha—holding on to truth—which had won freedom for India.

Today, for these same compelling reasons, countless millions of our Hindu brothers and sisters love and worship the compassionate Christ in their heart of hearts, though they may feel disinclined to belong to an institutional church. Such is the force of these magnetic words after two thousand years. They are ever old and ever new.

The motive behind the message is the perfect imitation of God. God is a Father who makes no distinction between friend and foe; who lets the sun shine and the rain fall on good and bad alike; who bestows His love and forgiveness upon those who do not really deserve them. True love does not worry about its requital, does not expect any reward. It is free from calculation and hidden self-seeking. I myself have experienced the truth of this message at a definite point in my ministry.

In a country parish where I had labored for almost ten years against great odds, many setbacks and disappointments, the people were noted for their pride of life and boastful cynicism. The beginning of my ministry among them had been an uphill task, and I had experienced moments of true despair because of their perverse ways and stubborn attitudes. Finally, with persevering prayer and hope against hope, I managed to win them over through one symbolic gesture that moved their hearts more than all my preaching and moral instruction ever had.

We were renovating the church for the parish jubilee celebration. A new altar was being built, and high above this altar, the tragic scene of the crucifixion was graphically depicted. Beneath it, the prayer of the dying Savior was written in bold letters: "Father, forgive them, for they do not know what they are doing."

That was the best sermon anyone could ever preach. The people were struck by the power of the message. Thereafter, a slow but perceptible transformation took place. People became more amenable to reason, more cooperative and helpful, and this resulted in a deeper union of hearts and minds. They began to appreciate the good work that was being done for their welfare in the fields of health, education and social services. Even today, many of them acknowledge their debt of gratitude and offer sincere regret for their stubborn attitudes of the past.

Father Kacumanu is engaged in parish work in Kankarakunta, Gundur, India.

Everything

Father Emile Brière

All I can say is that Jesus Christ is everything to me. He is my hope, my mercy. He is the Savior who redeems me from my sins. He is the joy of my heart who never abandons me even when I abandon Him: who never forgets me.

I never forget Him either. He is constantly present to my mind and to my heart. Whatever I have to do, I know I cannot do it without Him. Whenever I become anxious about anything, it is because I forget He is there, and does take care of everything, and will always take care of everything.

He doesn't make my life easy, but He certainly fills it with hope, joy and a deep ineffable happiness. He puts into my heart a constant awareness of the sufferings of my brothers and sisters in the world, and His Spirit moves me to cry out constantly, "Lord have mercy, Lord have mercy, Lord have mercy!"

He loves me and I love Him. In a world that is so unsure of itself, His word gives my life clear direction.

Yes, Jesus is everything to me.

Father Brière is a priest of Madonna House Apostolate in Combermere, Ont., Canada.

Nothing Can Come Between Us

Myra Berghane

O Jesus, how can I explain who You are in my life?
It's so easy to get into my head and call you Lord
and Savior, Second Person of the Trinity, sent by the
Father to free me from sin, alive today through Your
Holy Spirit. It's so hard to get away from the theology
books and uplifting pamphlets, and differentiate between knowing You in my head and knowing You in
my heart.

I'm tempted to explain *how* you came to be so much
a part of my life—the different renewal movements
within the church, my involvement in catechetics—but
then I'm back in my head again. The only thing that
really matters is that our relationship is different today
from what it was eight years ago—because You kept
pursuing me, and at some moment I surrendered and
allowed You to touch me with Your love.

I'd like to say, "No longer do I live, but You in me."
But I can't; not yet. You own more of me than You
did in the past, but not all; and I am pulled in two
because of it. Part of me longs to be totally Yours, to
know the freedom of detachment from myself and my
way of doing things, to trust You and Your Father
completely. And part of me is filled with fear of what
will happen if I do make the final surrender. So I run.

And You, the Hound of Heaven, pursue me. You have become the Great Pursuer.

When my life is settled and peaceful and I think our relationship is really "in a good place," You decide I must grow some more, must let go of yet another area of my life so that You can transform it. And that means death to part of me, so I flee and our nice stable relationship is upset. I find myself in the desert of Your silence, and I rail against You.

But even in the midst of my fury, I know You're there, behind me, waiting, until finally in exhaustion I stop running and collapse in the dust of my will, and You gently touch my heart, and as I die, I am born anew.

As I have come to know You in my heart, I have begun to experience You as Savior. You have shown me—not always gently—just how sinful I really am, so there can be no doubt about my need for You.

Instead of being a theological concept, "Savior" has become a necessity, a light shining in the darkness of my soul, where all the potential evils of the human race lie buried. If I am not an evil person, it is because of You and Your forgiving love; because You do forgive me, and that is the greatest freedom.

When I can see myself as a sinner, yet know I am loved and forgiven despite it, then I am free to love and accept myself. Once I do that, I can love and accept others. But this is so hard to believe! Human experience tells me that I must be punished for my sins, that I must earn love. I can't really believe You could love me just as I am—imperfect, broken; that I don't have to hide my darkness from You in fear of rejection.

Pursuer, Savior, Liberator, Lover, Healer of my heart, Light in my darkness—You are all of these, because I do believe *"nothing* can come between us and the love of God made visible in Christ Jesus our Lord" (Rm. 8:39). Nothing! Not even my human failings. Alleluia!

Myra Berghane, a former religion teacher, is a home-maker in Old Greenwich, Conn.

Who Would Comfort Us?

Francis P. Sing, Ph.D.

In September of 1949, I left China for the United States as a freshman in a college in New Jersey. I was late for college since some of my high-school classmates had already graduated from universities in China in June of that year.

When I came over here, I left behind my mother, my wife and two infant children, the youngest, a son, only one month old. I told my wife I would come home when our son was four. Unfortunately, my promise could not be kept because in late 1949, the communist conquest of China prevented me from returning, while also preventing my family from joining me in America, thus subjecting me to a long and painful separation of twenty-four years from my loved ones—a separation few people have ever experienced or can even comprehend.

During all those painful and lonely years, I remained cheerful and peaceful, knowing that whatever sufferings we must go through are but God's plans. We, His creatures, cannot fathom His mystery. Besides, wasn't it that which Jesus our Lord wants us to do? "Whoever wants to come after Me, let him deny himself and take up his cross, and follow me."

My cross, though heavy in terms of human sufferings,

was light compared with our Lord's passion and death. During that time, I often thought of Job: in comparison with his, my life was a joy. Job's faith in God and his obedience to God's will set an example for me to follow. Whenever I recited the Lord's Prayer, I would pause and ponder the meaning of "Thy will be done." Suddenly, the phrase became more meaningful and more intimate to me: "Yes, Thy will be done, O Lord!"

One additional lesson I have learned from those painful and lonely years is how insignificant and meaningless one's life may be if it is led independently from God's grace and support. This is precisely what Macbeth came to realize when he was surrounded by his enemies: "Life is but a walking shadow. . . . It is a tale told by an idiot, full of sound and fury, signifying nothing." Would he have thought in those terms had he not been driven by blind ambition to commit murder?

In May of 1973, I was allowed to return to my hometown in China, and by the mercy of God, my wife and two children were permitted to leave China with me for the States. They arrived here in November 1973. The miracle I had been praying for during those dark and lonely years finally came to pass. Alleluia!

Francis P. Sing is professor of economics at Georgetown University, Washington, D.C.

Who Is Jesus?

Ray Repp

That's a difficult question to answer in words.

It's a *personal* question I think every one has to face in his or her own way.

It's a *public* question that requires a profession of faith at some time in life.

It's a *private* question that everyone needs to consider alone.

For me, Jesus is more than just another historical figure. He is a Person who, I believe, came to give a sense of direction to the world. He's a Light that shines in the wilderness, as John the Baptist said; He's the Alpha and the Omega spoken of in the Book of Revelations.

He's all those things we are searching for—and my search is different from yours, and yours is different from mine—but at various moments in time we find ourselves walking hand in hand, in the same direction, on our way to discover an even better way to live, love and grow.

It's at these times I believe our search joins together and our concept of Jesus is the same.

Ray Repp, noted liturgical guitarist-composer, lives in Trumansburg, N.Y.

The Joy of Music

Karen Olson

Christ to me is love: He represents all I need. I am
a musician: for me, the meaning of Jesus in my life is
tied up with all the struggles and hard work the life of
an artist demands.

Once, when I was young and had hardly started
playing the violin, I stood before a mirror and told an
imaginary audience to go on towards all their goals
despite obstacles or contrary opinions—because this
was what I had done. At the time, however, no one, not
even myself, could have known the musician I would
become. I was only playing music in my mind.

Much later, when I was fourteen, I had the opportunity to study the viola and attended a summer music
camp. This was when my love for music was truly born.

All through high school I was very active. I was
principal viola in several orchestras, winning compe-
titions, obtaining scholarships and performing solos in
concerts, but I really didn't know what I was doing, or
what it was all about.

Before entering college, I received a full scholarship
to study in Switzerland. Everyone there was much
older and from a different world, contrasting with my
growing up in a minister's family in the Midwest.

Through much suffering I began to learn what real

love is. I had many powerful and painful experiences
and relationships—especially with a boyfriend—which
taught me to put my trust in God alone (a lesson I am
constantly learning in new ways).

I am now studying in the Juilliard School of Music,
and obtaining the best training I could hope for. I am
constantly using what God has taught me, and learning
more. It takes much faith to live on with uncertainty.
I was in dire need of financial aid, and never knew
where it would come from. I trusted the Lord, and He
provided, often in unexpected ways.

Through my music, I try to communicate to others
what is in my heart: the Lord's grace, His gifts and
love. The greatest reward for me is to see someone's
spirit lifted up by music, to see joy in the listener's eyes.

Yes, to me, Jesus is love; I hope to share this love in
my life through the gift of music.

*Karen Olson, a native of St. Paul, Minn., is a student
at the Juilliard School of Music in New York.*

Opening the Door
Father Robert Pelton, Ph.D.

Several years ago, I was spending a quiet October day in prayer, alone in a small cabin near some woods. The sun shone mildly on the fallen leaves. I was quiet, too, after many weeks of inner turbulence. Each time I opened the Bible, my eyes fell on words of consolation and mercy. All day long, the Lord spoke peace to me and bathed me in compassion.

Suddenly, in mid-afternoon, disarmed by such gentleness, I remembered the healing words of the Living One had spoken to the Laodiceans after chastising them: "Behold, I stand at the door and knock. If anyone hears my voice and opens the door, I will come in to him and eat with him, and he with me" (Rev. 3:20).

"Why not?" I thought. Hasn't He been knocking all day long? Why not be childlike enough simply to open the door to Jesus?

So, playfully, seriously, I got up, went to the door, opened it, and started to bow. I never finished the bow. Such a blast of joy exploded through the door that I was knocked to my knees. I felt as if I had been plunged into a nuclear furnace—or in the center of the sun.

I heard no words; I saw no visions; I only experienced, somehow, on my skin as well as in my soul this sunquake of joy bursting from the One who died and is

alive forever, from Jesus who walked into my solitude
to share with me the food He feasts on everlastingly
with the Father and the Spirit.

After that day, years of sorrow and healing, conversion and enlightenment would pass before it occurred
to me to answer simply, if asked about the Lord, "Jesus
is my joy."

Still, those few moments were a key that enabled me
to crack the inner code of my life. The certainty I was
made for joy sparked my decision to step across the
threshold into faith, into the invisible world of the
spirit, though I feared illusion and self-deception. The
fire of Jesus in the Eucharist left a radiance of joy on
my face that lasted for weeks after the Easter night of
my reception into the church. It was joy again that
overwhelmed me on that spring day I sensed Mary's
presence just behind me, and came to know why she is
called the Mother of Holy Joy. Even during the long
years of fear, when I refused to embrace the cross, and
yet felt my body curving toward the wholeness that lay
just beyond it, there was joy.

But why joy? I know no other Jesus than the One
whom the Catholic Church proclaims as Lord and God.
Jesus is the Messiah, Israel's Promised One, the Father's Gift of cleansing and rebirth, my Teacher, my
Master, my Friend, eternal Word made flesh for me
and in me.

The Father has made Him my Wisdom, my Justice,
my Healing, my Hope. He is my Beloved, and all I
am and have belongs to Him. The most passionate longing of my heart is to be able to say in all truth, "I no
longer live, but Christ lives in me."

Since love is the central Gospel reality, the Christian's source, way and goal, why not say Jesus is my Love, and leave it at that?

It is a question, I think, of that wholeness of love that lies on the other side of the cross. In solitude, Jesus has made the sun my friend, the moon and the stars my companions, the forests, the birds, the animals my family. He has stripped away my lies, exposed the darkest secrets of my selfishness, and there, in the darkness, has shown me the glory of His face.

At Mass, He has washed and fed me, and taught me to dance. In the community, He has done daily battle against the death-grip of my egotism, has taught me to see, and has given me brothers and sisters whose faces have become true icons of His. In my priesthood, He has shown me the pain of the world; and when I have made the least movement to embrace it, He has consoled me with the knowledge of the Easter already growing in that pain's womb. In the church, He has shared me with His Mother and His saints, so that when I am still and most alone with Him, I touch the men and women of every age who have come to love Him, and sense, just beyond the edge of my hearing, the song they sing before God's face.

The risen Jesus fills the universe with His presence, and where He is, I am too. In giving me all things, He gives me joy. But the more I experience creation transformed into joy by Jesus' love, the more I hear His promise of perfect joy, His own joy, the joy of His oneness with the Father.

Jesus wants to take me into this completion of love that lies at the very center of the cross, where He is wholly abandoned to the Father, where His flesh becomes the world's life. I don't always want to go so far: I am slow in giving my trust, even to the Lord—yet I will finally go because I hear His voice within me saying, "Come to the Father! Come into my joy!"

And so one day I will open the last door, and He who is my joy will take me into His joy—not out of my body, not out of this world, not away from my sisters and brothers (for even when I "die" I will lose them only to find them,) but into the center of the explosion, the unimaginable fullness of life, Fullness Itself: God.

Father Pelton, a priest of Madonna House Apostolate in Combermere, Ont., Canada, holds a doctorate in the history of religions and is an author.

Meaning and Hope

Sally Cunneen

My father died when I was on the threshold of difficult life-decisions. He had been ill, had prepared us as
much as he could, but the sharp, cold certainty of total
absence was almost too stunning to accept, and made
even less credible to me because my father died in lush
Florida where even mourners wear white.

Only the dark, unmistakable crucifix dominating the
altar during the old-style fire-and-fear funeral Mass
enabled me to take the slow steps that would lead to
acceptance. Jesus had gone before my father into this
unknown darkness, was with him now, and so human
death and separation had meaning, could coexist with
love. Impossible as it was to understand, it could be
suffered.

When I married, the liturgy included the words of
Jesus that this bond transcended natural ties. Our love
for one another was likened to the love of Christ for
the church. In His liturgical presence as mediator between the divine and the human, I found Jesus powerfully affirming our joy.

When my son died at eighteen after years of suffering, I felt the presence of Jesus in my life again. This
time I saw Him mocked, whipped and put to death
again in my son's affliction. Yet I knew Jesus had as-

sumed His own sufferings voluntarily, purposefully, while my son's agony seemed meaningless, inexplicable.

But slowly I came to see that Jesus had been here before, too. In His own suffering, had He not reached out even to my son, saying, "This too I have experienced for you."

There is hope, then, even where meaning seems absent. Finally, I realized Jesus was also asking me to create meaning in what remained of my life.

Comfort in the crisis of youth, affirmation of love and choice at adulthood, challenge and responsibility in the crisis of maturity—each with a sense of meaning and hope—these are the gifts I have received from Jesus. They have penetrated my most elemental human experiences with the assurance that even I, even there, share in the divine purpose of creation.

Sally Cunneen, author of "A Contemporary Meditation on the Everyday God" and other books, lives in West Nyack, N.Y., and is associate editor of Cross Currents.

Christ the Perfect Guide

Covington Hardee

The sin from which most evil flows is the sin of pride. By "pride," I do not mean the sense of self-worth and esteem that is necessary, desirable and sanctioned in the second of Jesus' new commandments. Rather, the sin of pride reflects an overweening human arrogance that ignores the majesty of earth and sky, that is willing to manipulate all or part of God's creation for personal gratification and aggrandizement.

All of us, to one degree or another, are afflicted by this form of what the Greeks called "hubris." Whether we engage in large acts of selfishness or small omissions of kindness, most of us are never really free from the enslavement of pride.

In Jesus Christ, we have the supreme example of the conquest over pride. The reminder of His life helps me each day to deal with the myriad choices and challenges I must face.

As a person charged with responsibility for making decisions that affect the lives and fortunes of many people, I need a daily injection of humility to counteract the dangerous tendencies of power. Jesus furnished us, for all time, with the ideal of a life lived for others. From small acts like the washing of the feet, to the ultimate sacrifice on the cross, He set forth the perfect

standard for our guidance. While none of us can hope
to attain His perfection, even modest progress in the
imitation of Christ can change our lives and often the
lives of those around us as well.

I thank God for the life of Jesus. Each time I bring
Him into my life and my thoughts, I know I am better
equipped to make right choices for myself, my family
and for the enterprise whose leadership God has entrusted to my care.

*Covington Hardee is president and chairman of the
board of the Lincoln Savings Bank of New York City.*

"My Lord and My God!"

Catherine de Vinck

It happened at a party many years ago. I don't remember the occasion, but I can still see the large number of people gathered around the long banquet table.

At the time I was a shy young girl, ill at ease and bored. The conversation turned to religion—or at least to that peculiar brand of religion which is willing to keep up external Christian traditions while looking down upon the church with skepticism and disdain.

I had kept silent, hardly interested in what people were saying. I, too, had become disenchanted with the church and saw it only as a crumbling ancient institution unable to respond to the problems of modern society.

Suddenly, I heard the young man sitting across the table from me make a disparaging comment about Jesus Christ. Feelings of intense anger shot through me like bolts of lightning. I protested, and he looked at me and said with a kind of smiling pity, "Well, my poor girl, if you still believe in fairy tales . . ."

He could not complete his sentence, for I had seized my glass full of water and hurled it in his face. Then I ran out of the room, up the stairs, and crumpled on the landing floor, sobbing and saying, "My Lord and my God!"

I knew then that Jesus was the Lord of my life.

Catherine de Vinck is a poet who lives in Allendale, N.J.

The "Not Nice" Jesus

Father Arthur McNally, C.P.

The Jesus I seem most anxious to call attention to is a Jesus who is, to put it succinctly, not "nice." We are so much aware of the kindness, gentleness, mercy and compassion of Jesus that we run the risk of losing sight of another Jesus, very much in evidence in the Gospels, who is wild, explosive and awesome. I refer to the Jesus who tore into the Scribes and the Pharisees, who turned on Peter and said, "Get behind me, you Satan!" The Jesus who cried out in frustration, "O unbelieving generation, how long will I be with you?"

When a man comes seeking help for his son, and says, "If you can do something. . . ." this Jesus roars in exasperation, "If! All things are possible to him who believes." This is the Jesus who can leave his family waiting at the edge of the crowd with these words: "Who is my mother? And who are my brothers and sisters? Whoever does the will of God is my mother and my sister and my brother!"

He loves little children, but he warns adults that anyone who scandalizes them would be better off if he had a millstone tied around his neck and were thrown into the sea. This Jesus has a lot to say about hell and demons. He advises, "If your eye is a problem to you, gouge it out! Better to enter the Kingdom of Heaven

with one eye than to spend your time in the fires of
Gehenna with two." He overturns the tables of the
moneychangers in the Temple; He curses fig trees that
have no figs (even when it is not the season for figs);
He cries out on the cross, "My God! My God! why
have You forsaken me?"

All the feelings "nice" people hide, this Jesus dis-
plays all over the place: anger, fear, sorrow, frustration. He hurts, upsets, irks, disappoints and frightens
people time and again. It is easy to understand why
this Jesus didn't last long in our world! The Lion of
Judah is a wild lion, not a tame one. And since faith
tells us He is alive within His followers, that means
grace does not always prompt us to be pussycats.

*Father McNally is the former editor of Sign maga-
zine and is now stationed at St. Paul's Monastery in
Pittsburgh, Pa.*

The Way, the Truth and the Life

Leo Joseph Cardinal Suenens

Too many Christians, baptized and confirmed in childhood, have not as adults ratified through a personal engagement the sacramental wealth dormant within them. What they lack is a true encounter with Jesus Christ; a discovery of His face, words, demands; a binding of themselves with Him existentially: for life and for death.

One day, while on his way, Jesus asked His disciples unexpectedly, "And you, who do you say that I am?" Peter's reply is well known.

The Master asks this direct and vital question from each new generation. There is no escape through generalities: it is quite useless to tell Him we acknowledge Him as the Master of our thoughts, an Example for our deeds, or a major Prophet—perhaps the greatest of all times. The fundamental question plunges into the heart like a sharp dagger that cannot be parried. And our Christian authenticity depends upon each individual's reply.

For Christianism is not primarily an "ism," a body of teachings, a rule of life. It is primarily a personal meeting with the risen Christ.

The more I advance in age, the more the face of Christ becomes luminous for me; the more His presence shows itself to be attentive, warm, delicate, permanent throughout the hazards of life. More and more every day, He appears to me not only as the One who comes to inspire and quicken my life, but as the One who is for me the safe Way, incarnate Truth and Life ever-renewed.

Little by little, He tends to become the breathing of my soul, to cover the whole horizon of my life like a rainbow over a landscape. He is everything at once—past, present and future—and that, both to me personally and to the universe.

Jesus Christ is the key word of creation and human history. He contains within Himself all the ages of the world, and particularly the sum total of Israel's hope: "The Law contains Christ within its womb." He is the complete answer to the expectation of the patriarchs, the prophets and Mary. He is God's promise, the knot of His covenant since the beginning.

In my own case, He came to enlighten my early years with the radiation of His power, like a dawning sun; He whispered to me the kind of words that make a destiny: "Come, and follow me!" Little by little, I discovered His close presence, like that of a friend; His sacramental action at the heart of the Church, particularly in the mystery of the Eucharist.

From there on, I have been able to live with increasing light, joy, certainty. It seemed to me I was discovering and verifying anew the lightning-truth of Jesus' words, "Whoever sees me sees the Father."

Jesus, a living image for His Father, has opened to me vistas concerning God which no philosopher has ever been able to reveal to me. I am quite willing to trade all the treatises on God I have read against the Gospel-page in which Jesus tells the story of the Prodigal Son. Through the psychology of the father watching for his son's return and receiving him with open arms, I can obtain a glimpse of the unbelievable love of our Father in heaven. It is enough to open for me a crack of heaven right here on earth; for I believe the greatest truth is to be found wherever the greatest love abides— and these few words contain my whole creed.

Cardinal Suenens, the retired Archbishop of Brussels, Belgium, is the author of a number of books.

The Servant-King

Linda Sabbath

A few years ago, when my children were about eight, ten and twelve, the eldest asked me if I would kill her if Christ asked me to do so. I explained to her that Christ was pro-life and would never ask me such a thing, so therefore it was a non-question.

The three of them argued with me and demanded a straight answer. Because I was not absolutely certain of what to say, I became evasive and they in turn persistent. I never did tell them, but I was forced to tell myself, yes—I would do exactly what Abraham did with Isaac. And on the sacrificial altar of my heart, I placed my own self and my three children. This became the greatest step I had yet taken, and it led to years of intoxicating and rapturous joy; a thunderous beating of love that ravished my body and mind.

Faster than the speed of sound or light, I entered many heavens and realms of paradise. Christ was my Bridegroom and I His bride, blinded by His tumultuous love that was both gentle and violent, and dissolved me into His being, into all of His creatures, into His entire creation—down to the smallest insect, down to the trash of garbage cans.

Every person became a saint, every fleck of dust was sacred, and every sound—from a bird song to a car honk—became music of praise to His glory. For years, my heart ached and pained with love for Him and from Him, and my mind fought and rebelled because I was yet forced to exist on this earth, tied by a silver cord that would be cut only by my next death, my next birth.

My Bridegroom became my Father who taught me, guided me, reprimanded me; my Gardener who pruned me, forced me to greater maturity and more abundant flowering. He became my King of Kings and Lord of Lords, and I spent many years marveling at both His greatest and most minute creations. My mind reeled more and more as I came to realize that I, too, was one of His divine creations. No longer was I a Canadian woman with a social insurance number. I became a citizen only of His heavenly kingdom, beyond male and female, beyond Greek and Jew. On days of jubilation, my King became my Dancing Partner; on days of trial and sorrow and pain, He became my Physician and Comforter, my loving Mother.

When I could stop staggering under the love poured into my body and spirit, and the light that illuminated creation before my eyes, I was seized with the tireless desire to bring others to the knowledge of His gratuitous and rapturous love. My husband and I founded the Thomas Merton Center for Contemplative Prayer. In the ten years of its existence, we have observed our King lavishing His love and His gift of contemplative prayer upon any human who asks for them. We have seen it offered, and accepted by criminals, psychotics and mentally retarded people. My mind still reels, my finite mind staggers, my heart bursts in pain and love.

The King of Kings, the Creator of our world is now

my Servant: He is the Servant of the entire human race.
Only a servant, and only the lowliest, is available night
and day, every week of the year, every moment of existence, to do his master's bidding. This Servant is constantly available to the whole family of man, ready to
give us gifts of attention, love, guidance. No trade-
union laws exist to limit His service to us; He never
rests. He is fully available to every one of us, at any
time, under any circumstances, regardless of how inso-
lent, rude, cruel or evil we may be. Has there ever
lived a King so totally enslaved to his subjects? I am
prostrate in the dust before Him, the humblest janitor
in His palace.

"I mean to sing of Jahweh all my life,
I mean to play for my God as long as I live.
May these reflections of mine give him pleasure,
As much as Jahweh gives me."

(Psalm 104)

*Linda Sabbath is the founder of the Thomas Merton
Center in Magog, Quebec, Canada.*

A Christ to the Neighbor

Roland Bainton, Ph.D., D.D.

I was startled when I read Luther's word that a Christian must be a Christ to the neighbor. The assertion presents no difficulty if it means simply that one should love the neighbor as the self, love the enemy, embrace the prodigal, cherish little children, go the second mile, wash the disciples' feet, and put loyalty to God above family and state. This is simply the imitation of Christ, trying to do what He did and enjoined.

But Christ, we believe, has done more for us than all this. Christians have always applied to Him verses from the fifty-third chapter of Isaiah: "Surely he has borne our griefs and carried our sorrows. . . . He was wounded for our transgressions. He was bruised for our iniquities. The Lord has laid on him the iniquities of us all and by his stripes we are healed."

Can a Christian assume the guilt of others and feel in any way involved with sins not personally committed? Can the Christian take to himself the sins of society or the state? The answer is yes.

After the Second World War, I met some people in Germany who at the time of the Holocaust did not know what was happening. They knew Jews were being deported, but they believed it was to camps like those we had for the Nisei. When the truth came to light, these people felt shame for the crimes of their government.

Likewise in the United States we should feel shame that our country was the first to drop the atom bomb. The actual number of casualties may have been less than that resulting from earlier saturation bombings, but the new weapon was more cruel and ominous for the future. As Americans, we must assume the guilt of our nation and endeavor to redress this wrong.

On the personal level, can parents assume the guilt of their children, and the children that of their parents? Again, they can. There is a sharing of guilt, not specifically, but in a broad way: a sharing in shame, feeling, and as much restitution as can be made. The sins of our loved ones are laid upon us, and ours upon them. By our stripes, by their stripes, there is mutual healing.

Dr. Bainton has been Titus Street Professor of Ecclesiastical History at Yale University. A specialist in Reformation history, he is the author of "Here I Stand, a Life of Martin Luther," and "What Christianity Says About Sex, Love and Marriage," among other books.

I Sought Him Whom My Heart Loves

Rochelle Greenwood

The question, "For you, who is Jesus Christ" can be answered in part with the biblical quotation, "I sought him whom my heart loves" (Song of Songs, 3:1).

Since childhood, I loved to stop in our parish church after school and pray at the statues of the Immaculate Mother and the Sacred Heart. Some days I would spend more time with one, other days with the other. For me, there was no theological problem as to which one should receive the most attention. One was the Mother, the other the Son—and the nickel or dime spent on an occasional vigil light was a joyous sacrifice, as are offerings of love.

Grade and high school passed. College began. When big or little difficulties came my way, it was to Jesus, Mary and Joseph I ran for consolation and encouragement. My belief was that just their listening hearts were all that mattered, hearts that cared about sorrows.

Yes, since childhood, I have been seeking "him whom my heart loves." Now, in adult life, I have come to know from experience another line of the Song of Songs: "I sought, but did not find him."

When God knows someone is in earnest about loving Him, He is paradoxically "available" and "not available." He does not make Himself immediately accessible. Oh yes, He offers Himself in the sacraments, especially the Eucharist. But He is not like a cup one can pick up from a shelf: He is within, yet His presence cannot always be "commanded," at least not always in the manner we would choose. Since He is God, He can determine just how and how much to manifest His presence. It is His prerogative. He is the keenest hide-and-seek player I have ever met!

Once he has been "found" and yet is ever more deeply "sought," a conclusion from the Song of Songs is fitting:

> "Set me like a seal on your heart,
>   like a seal on your arm.
> For love is strong as death,
>   jealously relentless as Sheol.
> The flash of it is a flash of fire,
>   a flame of Yahweh himself.
> Love no flood can quench,
>   no torrents drown."

Rochelle Greenwood is a staff member of Madonna House Apostolate in Combermere, Ont., Canada.

The Poet-Creator

Archbishop Joseph Raya

When I first read the question, "For you, who is
Jesus Christ?" my whole being sang a hymn of joy for
the opportunity to put into words what was so bright
and clear and alive in me. Yet, words are an inade-
quate means for telling who a person is—and much
more so when that person is Christ. But when there is
a song within us, we must sing it out with our own
vibrations, deficient as it may be.

For me, Jesus Christ is first of all and above all my
God, my Savior and my Lord. He is God, the God of
God, the very God of the very God. He is God, Creator
and Possessor of the whole universe. In the language
of my Greek Church, the Maker and the Poet have
the same root.

I believe in one God, Father Almighty poetizing
creation. For my God, creating is creating a poem. He
composed a poem and called it "Heaven"; he composed
another and called it "Earth," and yet another he
called "Stars."

My God composed an infinity of poems. The most
splendid of them he called "Persons": cherubim and
seraphim, archangels and angels, and finally man and
woman. In the human person, God summarized His
power and beauty and concentrated the miracles of the

universe, uniting in them the vision of the faraway
heavens and the functions of the smallest atoms. Man-
woman is the mirror in which God reflects His great-
ness and His glory. The human person in the flesh was
destined to become His dwelling place; His very self
was to be revealed in that flesh—which then became
the channel of the return of the whole creation to its
origin: God Himself.

All the poems of my God! Every single poem and
every part of every poem is ever fresh, ever new, ever
alive, singing and dancing and radiating light, and the
life and warmth of the resurrection. Every poem reflects
God's goodness!

The Jews adore my God, the Moslems proclaim
Him. Since the millions of years human beings have been
reflecting, and walking on their two feet, every one of
them has stood in awe and admiration before Him.
They have called their God by many names: "Father,"
"Mother," "Nature," "First Principle of Motion," "Supreme Being," "Eternal Art," "Beauty," "Love." Many
are the names, but the reality is One. My God indeed
answers all these names—and infinitely more. A name
is a mask, but a smile reveals a person. My God is a
person: Jesus.

God can be neither induced nor deduced from philo-
sophical logic. Even the Bible contains no imposed
formula concerning Him: a prophetic Word opens
yesterday and today in view of a better experience of
a God who never ceases revealing Himself.

Confucius had a glimpse of Him, and also the
Buddha. Ancient human cultures, Persian, Egyptian,
Chinese, African, American as well as the Greek and

the Roman, each had a glimpse of the "Incomprehensible God." Mohammed had a brilliant insight of Him, and Moses was shaken by His reality. Each one of the prophets of old and each event in Israel's history uncovered a new aspect of God. And He kept on revealing Himself—until one day, when humanity was ready "to see his face and not die," He joined heaven to earth and became Man.

God became real man, a man who wept and smiled, a man who suffered and who thrilled with joy, a man who hungered and thirsted, and whose flesh vibrated with all the love, tenderness, disappointments and triumphs of our humanity. The One who bears all names became a human face and was named Jesus. The Invisible became visible, and the Untouchable assumed human flesh, touchable and touching. God is no longer "The One Out There," a vague dispenser of pie-in-the-sky, but "Emmanuel," "God-With-Us," a companion whose human voice carries and reveals the secrets of heaven.

In Jesus, the abstract becomes concrete reality; God takes on a smiling countenance, a face that glows with light and goodness. Since Jesus possesses the fullness of divinity, He fulfills it in His personal experience and moves in it freely, joyously, easily. He uses the most daring language to describe God. "Father" is but a name; "Daddy" is a face. Jesus calls His Father "Abba," "Daddy."

God is not "that old bachelor who lives in boredom and loneliness" whom Nietzsche mistakenly took for the God of the Christians. He is "Abba," eternally generating the Son and breathing the Spirit. We believe in a God who is Father-Son-Spirit; we do not count "One" or "Three." We believe in One-in-Three, or Three-in-One; we point to an inexpressible relationship between the Persons; we proclaim that there is an active inner life in God: fecundity, generosity, giving-receiving; that there is Love; that He is Love.

Since Jesus is God, one with the Father and the Spirit, He too is God of God, the very God. He thus reveals the fullness of the Godhead. Since Jesus is Man, one with humanity, one with man-woman, He also reveals the value of the human race. Through His flesh, all men and women become His brothers and sisters. He proclaims that all men and women came from the heart of God, the "Abba." Hence their origin is divine. He assumed human flesh and united all men and women to Himself. Hence their condition and value are divine. He went up to heaven and established all human flesh—all men and women—on God's throne. Hence their destiny is divine. The proclamation of this revelation by Jesus Christ is called the "Good News," or "Gospels."

God's poem goes well beyond human logic because it expresses His freedom and beauty. Christ wanted human life to be a poem like His own, overflowing with freedom, renewal, resurrection and redemption. He Himself celebrated them all in His flesh.

My personal relationship with Jesus Christ in the present time is different from that of the Apostles in theirs. After Christ-God returned to heaven, He sent the Spirit to continue the revelation of the Godhead. Indeed, He never ceases to reveal Himself: He will be unfolding the veil of His goodness and love as long as

He remains God, the Father and Lover of humanity.

For the Apostles and Disciples at Emmaus, Jesus was a simple companion; with the unfolding of revelation, we now understand what was beyond the comprehension of His contemporaries. Jesus Christ is not a "Star," a "Hero," a "Prophet"—or even a "Super-Star": He is all that, and yet infinitely more: He is God, Savior and Lord.

My God, my Savior and my Lord, in Your presence I stand in awe, admiration and deep adoration.

Archbishop Raya, now associated with Madonna House Apostolate in Combermere, Ont., Canada, was formerly Archbishop of the Melkite Eparchy of Aka, Haifa, Nazareth and All Galilee.

A Personal Gospel

Sister Miriam Devlin, M.D.

It is awesome to presume to have walked in the company of Jesus of Nazareth for some thirty odd years—and then to be asked for the story of this journey. To speak of that which all too often I have left unspoken demands serious reflection. Perhaps from time to time all of us should write our own gospel, our witness to Jesus Christ, the anointed Lord.

In all births, there is great mystery, so the initial call to follow Christ in my life is hazy and unclear as to detail, but it is strong as to purpose and form. From the first, I wanted to be, not only a religious nun, but a missionary. During childhood, my encounter with the divine had taken the form of great devotion to the Mass and to the Blessed Sacrament. Yet, there was little in my behavior that would have betrayed my inner desire for I guarded it with the utmost secrecy.

When I had come of age to enter the convent, I suddenly was made aware that a commitment to Christ would have to be made on His own terms. Three weeks before entering religious life, I lost the greatest love I had ever had. My mother died suddenly, ending the dialogue between us and leaving many things unsaid. But the Good Lord does not empty a vessel except to refill it, so He gave me His Mother in the form of a deep spiritual attachment to her, and of adoption into a community dedicated to her Immaculate Conception.

The journeys of my ministry resembled those of most missionaries. We are all patterned after the great St. Paul, "in journeying often. . . ." by car, train, plane, bus and also by bicycle, pedicab, ferryboat, donkey and even on foot. While trying to follow in the Master's footsteps, I discovered the inconveniences of having "no place to lay one's head." But contact with other peoples and cultures gave me more than I could return: I was growing and maturing in Christ. The repeated receiving and letting go—of family, friends, countries and cultures—served as a preparation for a time when much more would be required, for the journey through one's own private gospel ultimately leads to the Passion.

There are many trips to Jerusalem, many encounters with Christ, but one was scheduled to end for me in the Passion-Resurrection. I knew this was to be, but the reality of it never clearly surfaced—until I found myself on a course which I could not control because the situation was in control of me. During this time of trial and suffering, I could see the Passion, particularly as it began to be played out in the events of my life.

I had experienced Christ's presence but He was now hidden for me. Darkness, fear, panic took over, heightened because of my own sensitivity to a state of inner turmoil. A sense of abandonment and betrayal engulfed me, enabling me to share in some small way the anguish of Jesus in the Garden. From that point on, He had ac-

cepted as His Father's will whatever would happen to
Him. I was not so strong, but did not have to be, as
long as I could hold to the fact that my weakness was
an opportunity for His strength to show.

While inching through one's inner passion, there are
many deaths one must endure—of mind, body, emo-
tions or spirit; many denials of self that seem to wash
over each other. If all of them had struck together, survival would have been impossible.

Jesus seemed far away, but suddenly, the Father was
there. For the first time in my life, I perceived the presence of "The God of the Mountain," El Shaddai—in
clouds descending, thunder and lightning, all of nature
bending to His almighty hand: Jesus had pointed the
way to the Father—an awesome thought, yet wonder-
filled!

It is the Father's will that must be fulfilled. I only
have to push onward, guided along the path the Lord
has traveled before me. Soon the storm breaks, the
darkness recedes, the stone rolls back and the great
light appears: creation falls into place. The Lord finds
no delight in death, for He is the God of the Living.
Life is the message He brings; His desire is to enlighten us with His light.

Christ is related to me in that I am called upon to
follow, not only discipleship, but also the divine will—
to be sister-brother-mother to Him. But He is more.
He is the final Passion-Resurrection event towards
which my life is moving; He takes away from me a
heart of stone, to give me a human heart that my love

may become real—for there is no other commandment than to love.

Sister Miriam Devlin is a medical doctor and a member of the Missionary Sisters of the Immaculate Conception stationed at Bucksport, Maine.

Meeting God

Father Joseph McFarlane, S.J.

To me, Jesus is the Son of Mary and the Son of God—of Mary in His human nature, of God in His divine nature. He is the Lord's revelation of part of Himself. He tells me that God understands and loves our human life—that He loves us and is part of this human life, and is therefore accessible and comes so close to us I can approach Him.

The human qualities of Jesus I know partly from Scriptures, and partly from descriptions of those who knew Him personally, either as witnesses as He walked this earth, or as the recipients of revelations in every age since then. Not only was He a real man at one point in time: He *remains* close to me and to every other human being—not only in the culture of His time and place, but in every other culture too. He not only created all men and women and loves them, but He also wants to live in and with them.

Because of His humanity, I know I can share my humanity with Him as He shares His with me. Because I can never comprehend His divinity, He is a mystery. But that part of my humanity which enables me to reach out in loving friendship with Jesus can reach God and be accepted by Him.

Through this meeting of humanity and divinity in

Jesus, I feel welcome and called upon to meet God myself through Jesus—and also to meet God, really though mysteriously, through every other human being.

For me, the most thrilling and challenging and rewarding experience of life is to be invited into God's presence, wherever He may be and however He chooses to reveal Himself.

God's mystery and the real sense of closeness to Him through Jesus makes me ready to face death whenever it comes, because I believe I will then see Him as He really is—and that is what I want more than anything else.

Father McFarlane, now retired and living in Boston, is a former editor of Jesuit publications and former national promoter of the Sodality movement.

All the Way

Allison Rose Nichols

Jesus Christ—
  not static or confined to my perception of Him.

He is GOD—
  bigger than all my insights and words.
  Everywhere in creation and goodness,
  my humble faculties find Him unexplainable, yet
    central.
  So I attempt to comprehend,
    name,
    claim
    who He is to me now.

REDEEMER—
  My nature is sin.
  The nature of Christ's life and death offers forgive-
    ness.
  I need His arms again and again.
  I rediscover that His trust alone frees me to live
    positively, freshly, boldly.

LOVER—Strength.
  He doesn't just remove my pain,
    know my hurts,

care for wounds:
He *created* me beautiful;
He *recreates* me gently.
Both are affirmations of love.

LORD—Much more than a warm sheltering hug.
His answer of forgiveness sets me free to run.
He's my Master Questioner, an example of love not
demanding,
yet invoking my works in devotion to follow his
way.
All the way.

*Allison Rose Nichols is a student at Luther College,
Decorah, Iowa.*

Saving Us From Ourselves

Shirley DeWitt Poore

One night at dinner a friend of ours, tracing history, stopped at the question, Who is Jesus Christ? Did we believe He was the Son of God?

As I listened, only one thought came to mind: he has never met the Person of Jesus. I knew who Jesus was, but not through my intellect. Rather, having been face-down, lacking all hope, struggling for some sense of identity, I had reached out from my depths and begged for faith.

I had known Jesus in my childhood, very simply, unquestioningly. Later, I became enraged by what He asked of us. Hurt, frightened, in despair, I questioned: "Where is this God of love, this God of mercy, this God who brings peace to the broken-hearted, water to the thirsty?"

I felt like the woman with hemorrhage in the Gospel story: If only I could touch the hem of His garment! With the Samaritan woman at the well, I asked for the living waters of faith. Slowly, with painful steps, I regained hope, faith in myself, faith in Jesus.

I have discovered Him again and again, each time differently, each time with new questions. I see Him as the Person who brings us out of the darkness of ourselves. "Behold, I make all things new!" I see Him as the Word that changes the impossible to the possible; the One who can bring forth new life, no matter how painful or desolate the circumstances.

He is the "Yes!" the affirmative, the positive. He helps us to let go of our idols one by one, to peel off the layers of self-deception. He beckons us to enter self-knowledge. He leads us to healing, to prayer, to the desert. He leaves us open-ended, with a future rich in possibilities transcending human life.

Knowing Him revolutionizes our existence: perspectives change, life can no longer be seen with the same eyes. We become listeners to the divine, hearing His voice in the most unlikely places. We may meet Him at the Communion rail, yes, but also at a Saturday night gathering with friends. We see Him anew in our brothers and sisters. We hear His words: "By this will all men know you: that you love one another."

Jesus invades all of life. "I have come that you may have life and have it more abundantly." We cannot categorize Him, place Him, diminish Him, assign Him a role. He moves wherever He will, often among those who say they do not believe but are seeking honestly. He passes in all places among us sinners.

He is with us, He is within us, the Good News present despite all evil. Even when all may seem hopeless, His believers know He will overcome and save them from themselves, for His presence has invaded the earth: the Word made Flesh!

Shirley DeWitt Poore, a homemaker, lives in Chantilly, Va.

Being for Others

Tom Tweed

Like many of my peers, I cut myself off from the church during my first year in college. It was not so much a "decision" as a "fading away." The reasons were both articulated and unformulated, but they were many—clericalism, sexism, over-emphasis on authority and orthodoxy, and the failure to apply Jesus' ethics to social concerns. This had been my experience in my parish and my community.

The summer of my sophomore year, however, my perceptions changed. I was working in a national park in California, and there I came across a small group of Christians who seemed to believe in the existence of one Spirit, but expressed in many different yet equal gifts. They listened to my doubts with respect and toleration. They seemed to be living by what I had previously heard about Christian ethics.

In this group, I encountered an "incarnation" of a just and loving God. This experience gave me hope—hope that I could be a Christian and still retain intellectual integrity, hope that Jesus' vision for humanity could actually be put into practice in the everyday.

I came to believe that the inequalities within the church, its apparent apathy towards suffering and injustice, and its largely authoritarian character could (to a large extent) be amended. Most importantly, I came to believe that Jesus' vision was reasonable, responsible and realistic. Since then, my life at its best has been an attempt to understand Jesus' message and to live by it.

All this is not to say that I am no longer outraged and hurt by the church. In fact, the question of whether to remain in the Catholic Church is an abiding one for me. Many of the wrongs that engendered my earlier discontent remain. The difference is that I now know other people in the church who see the problems as I do, and are working to alleviate them.

In any case, I call myself a Christian. I do so because I have experienced the power of Jesus' life of "being for others," and the hope of His message of peace, justice and human liberation.

Tom Tweed, a graduate of Harvard Divinity School, is a member of the faculty at St. Andrew's School in Boca Raton, Fla.

"Christ on Every Face I See"

Susan Keffler Vignos

"Christ before me, Christ behind me, Christ on every face I see," says an old hymn, the Breastplate of St. Patrick. When Pope John Paul II told the people of France to "love Jesus," did he mean that we need to recognize the God-Man in each other?

* * *

Cell biologists today think that we humans are gatherings of eukaryotes, the descendants of symbiotic prokaryotes. Jesus—God-made-Man—told us something we can see with an electron miscroscope: we are all one.

In the course of our development as a species millions of years after the appearance on earth of *Australopithecus Afarensis,* the famous "Lucy" and her kin, God entered into His creation as one of us: Jesus. At a certain time, God-made-Man entered into history, and entered into the course of our survival.

* * *

As a child, I recited the All Souls' Day *Toties quoties* indulgenced prayers for all my dead relatives. Then, each year, I prayed again for the most unloved dead I could think of, Adolf Hitler, and later Joseph Stalin. It seems to me the ultimate horror to be cast out of human caring as were these two. Thirty years later, I still feel that however horridly a person behaved, it would be even more destructive to remove him from my personal concern.

Jesus told us that we are one, that caring is of our essence, necessary to being human. What He taught in this regard is borne out now in our study of biology, paleontology and sociology. Caring is necessary to our survival. The message is always the same: each one of us must be personally involved in the good of others.

Jesus came into time in time. Today, as we tinker with earth's ecological structure and with our own fragile species, it is a time when we feel uneasy, rightfully fearing our self-destruction.

With all this in mind, I look into the eyes of each person I meet, looking for the Savior. "Christ on every face I see."

Susan Keffler Vignos is a homemaker who lives in North Canton, Ohio.

What Jesus Did

Father John J. Demkovich

I thought I knew Jesus throughout most of my life. Now I realize there is always more to discover about His life in us. If you ask me now, at age forty-seven, ordained fifteen years and pastor of a parish, what Jesus means to me, I would have to say I am learning that Jesus wants to live in me, to do through me the things He did during His life on earth.

The thought struck me recently that as Jesus walked the streets of the Holy Land for about three years, He spent most of His time—and in fact, enjoyed—chatting with the ordinary folk, lifting them up spiritually, healing them if they needed that ministry. This was His life and daily routine, and He had only three years to carry out the public mission laid upon Him by His Father.

His days were filled with expert teaching, uplifting conversations, and the burning desire to make people want what He had to offer them. We have no record of His writing letters or books. He was constantly in direct contact with the people, and would withdraw only when it was time for Him to commune with His Father in prayer.

Jesus couldn't stand to see people lonely and desolate, people hurting physically, emotionally, mentally.

He knew He could remedy their troubles. And He did, as long as their faith allowed them to receive Him.

Why should I see *my* life as being any different from that of Jesus? As a pastor, I am privileged to arrange each day's visits to people, lay hands in prayer for healing and blessing, bring them the words and sacraments of Life, and try to do what is often so difficult, yet joyful—to be there, available when anyone is in need.

If Jesus really wants to use my human nature—the make-up of body and soul I call "me"—all I've got to do is let Him do so. Isn't He living with me each day? Doesn't He want to use me to do the same things He did when He ministered to others? When He ministered to His Father from the hills and valleys of this earth?

What a thought to realize I can give Jesus the joy of using me to do the exact same work He was doing while He lived on earth! It's like lending myself to Him, and then letting Him take over as thoroughly as possible, letting Him use my hands, feet, voice, mind, heart, so He can glorify His Father all over again on earth.

Does Jesus feel like healing this sick person? The name of Jesus is the healing name. I identify with Jesus, call upon His name in boldness, and expect Him to keep His promise to work in and through me. It seems so simple: it really is!

Wasn't that a major part of the Father's "master plan"? That once His Son had died and risen from the dead, He would create millions of replicas of Himself by taking over people's lives in baptism, letting His own Spirit possess and vivify them, and have His Spirit direct these fortunate people to lay down their lives in submission, making Jesus their absolute Lord? Their joy will be to be present *WHEREVER* Jesus wants them, *WHENEVER* He wants them there, *AS LONG* as He wants them, and only *BECAUSE* He wants them.

This kind of vision of the meaning of Jesus in a person's life has freed me from things that don't matter: cares, pursuits, possessions, attachments He hadn't planned for me. How true that the more Jesus is in charge, the more liberated from self we become! Jesus is still searching for myriads of people who want Him to be truly Lord of their lives.

Father Demkovich is pastor of St. Mary's Assumption parish in Passaic, N.J.

A New Life

Noreen Drukker

Christ is gentle. He gave Himself to the world lovingly, freely. However, in order to rejoice in the exaltation of Easter, one must pass with Him through the pain of Calvary. Only after such an experience can one appreciate the Lord in a mature way.

The beginning of my transformation came with the shock of a divorce and a court battle over the custody of my child. My days were dark and depression became a constant companion. I was unable to realize what Christ was teaching me through this trial. I felt alone, full of self-pity, unaware that this pain would pass and I would be reborn.

Yet, over and again, Christ would touch my heart. I found Him in nature, in the quiet clearness of dawn and in the stillness of starry nights. I spoke to Him in prayer and meditation. But most of all, Christ comforted me through the compassion of my friends. Their caring enabled me to accept my struggle for a new identity. I became not only a stronger person, but a more mature Christian.

Christ said that we must follow Him; He meant we must walk with Him along the way to Calvary as well as rest with Him in the green meadows of Palestine.

We accept the total commitment to experience joy and sorrow.

Today, I am remarried to a marvelous man. He is an attentive and loving husband and a wonderful step-father to my daughter. There is a saying, "Let go and let God." My husband and I believe that Christ gently guided us toward one another to begin a new life, our own earthly Easter.

Noreen Drukker, a homemaker, lives in Montclair, N.J.

Personal and Universal Love

Joan Bel Geddes

Jesus plays several important roles in my life:

■ As I read about Him in Scriptures, He is the most original, interesting, magnetic Person in history.

■ As I meditate about the implications of His unique relationship with God the Father, He fills me with worshipful awe.

■ As I watch Him, a resurrected, potent influence, I wonder at His power over our dramatically changed world two thousand years after His short life.

For me, He is a reliable personal friend, guiding me through confusing, distressing moments, always coming up with the message or example I need when I need it—not pompous or abstract, but simple, succinct, loving, saying with a few eloquent words or a vivid parable exactly what I need to hear—and apply—at any given moment.

Above all, I am endlessly grateful for the amazing way He invented to stay close to me and to people of all nations and eras through the Eucharist: transforming material food and drink into spiritual nourishment, enabling us to experience at a level beyond speech the most sublime, intimate, tender, broad outreach, up-reach, in-reach, down-reach, everywhere-reach!

When I receive Communion, I feel incredibly close

to my Creator and to the Holy Spirit who illuminates sincere people all over the world. Each one of us, embraced and made one in the All, bathed, swathed in love that is simultaneously personal and universal: "I in you, and you in me!"

Despite how much Jesus means to me, I am not a religious imperialist. I don't look down on people who don't know Him. If they find inspiration and wisdom from other sources, I rejoice. I believe they may arrive through other channels at the truths Jesus exemplifies for me. He said there were other "sheep" and other "mansions" in His Father's house. I am sure He loves them all, and I thank Him and try to imitate Him.

Joan Bel Geddes lives in New York and is the author of the best-seller "To Barbara With Love" and other books.

He Comes Again and Again

Jim Murray

As a young man, I had abandoned Christ. One night, I dreamed that a black figure, an evil one, was trying to come in through my window to seize me. The more I struggled, the greater his success, until he invaded the room and grappled with me. When he had his hands on my throat, I instinctively began to pray, "Our Father who art in heaven. . . ." He was defeated! I was amazed that deep in my unconscious mind, at a time I had forsaken Christ, this would have been the solution—and the response.

Over the years, I have learned that although I am narcissistic, I do not love myself as Christ loves me. My self-love is finite and it wavers. My relationship with Christ has tended to parallel my level of self-love or self-hate at any time. When I find it difficult to excuse myself for sin, often I have neglected to ask His forgiveness. I have dulled my mind to the awareness of His presence and have moved away from Him.

I have found, though, that He, Love, is patient. When I ask, I receive.

I am like Peter: I profess my love, but the light flickers at varying levels of intensity. Oftentimes when the cock crows, tears well up with my recognition that I have denied Him yet again.

But the hunger and the thirst grow. I must taste His flesh and drink His blood, again and again; and I must watch and listen and wait. For He comes, and again, and again. If we but call, He comes. His love is balm. It heals. At the same time, it gives us added insight, new pain, as we become newly aware of our shortcomings.

Jim Murray lives in Bethesda, Md. Formerly a top administrator with the Washington, D.C., Police Department, he retired as evaluation manager for the Civil Service Commission in 1979.

Unfolding Mystery

Betty Powers Smith

When I asked myself, "Who, for me, is Jesus Christ?" my immediate thoughts were: He is a friend, brother, counselor, teacher, confidant. . . . But I find that too abstract: His presence is both larger and more intimate. I can describe it only in terms of experience with Him, the times I turn to Him. There are no categories for that Presence.

As I wait for sleep at night, sometimes I think of a clumsy or embarrassing word or action I regret, or something important I failed to say or do. Almost automatically, I call, "Jesus!" as though needing His reassurance that I'm okay. And I do need that!

Often before breakfast I sit at a window and meditate. I may read a Gospel passage and then sit with Him, see Him there, perhaps with the blind beggar Bartimaeus. I imagine His voice as He says, "What do you want me to do for you?" and marvel at His ready love. Or I take a favorite passage, such as, "If one of you hears me calling and opens the door, I will come in to share his meal, side by side with him." I listen for His message to me as I repeat the words or phrases one by one, letting each sink in. We are together.

With Him, I began to understand what forgiveness means, what He meant when He answered Peter's ques-

tion, "How many times should we forgive?" with the
words, "Seventy times seven!" Over a period of time,
I had made a point of picking one person or another
and going back to an occasion of hurt—mine or theirs.
I could see Him there with us, and letting His love flow
through me, I would replay the scene. Or I would
simply let His forgiving love dissolve my guilt or resentment.

I have friends with whom I pray aloud and study the
Bible. We feel the presence of Christ. As we pray, His
Spirit gives us the words to express deep feelings and
insights. As we read and discuss a scriptural passage
and apply it to our own situation, His message often
becomes quite clear and personal.

He is also in the person I find hard to accept. Sometimes succeeding, more often failing, I try to find Him
there. When I let myself be vulnerable in relationships,
He is there. He is in the friend in need and in the friend
who comforts me in mine. He is in a lonely acquaint-
ance, in a beggar on a city street. I used to look
knowingly at such beggars, figuring many could be
fakes. I seldom stopped to give them anything. Then
I wondered, "What of the needy ones I may be passing
by?" So now, I take no chances.

When I put things, preoccupations at the center of
my life, I seem to lose Christ, although I am sure He
is there, even in my indifference. When I make people
important in my life, I am more directly aware of His
presence. I am learning unevenly, with many errors
and falls—but learning. He teaches, leads, loves with
subtlety.

When I feel powerless, I turn to him and receive His power.

I experience Him in the Eucharist, and this experience is at the core of my life. I come to it in praise and thanksgiving, but mostly in need. I come with the gift of myself—the gift of a weakness, a failure, a need, a joy, an accomplishment. I put it on the altar to be offered with the bread and wine, to be raised up and made holy. I ask Him to join my gift to His gift of himself to the Father. And so my life, in all its messiness, has meaning.

He has taught me that the cross was not a tragedy, but a triumph; that resurrection comes only after death; that to die is to live. He reminds me with the words, "Do this in memory of Me," that when I bring to the Eucharist the smallest deaths, the letting go, the stepping off in faith into the darkness, I am raised up through Him and with Him—to Life. With this truth, He has given me the wisdom to know what to do at difficult points in my life; and He has given me the courage to do it.

Trying to sum up who Jesus Christ is in my life, I found myself tripping over theological phrases. I reject them together with the neat categories and roles they imply. His reality is none of these. He is an unfolding, living Mystery!

Betty Powers Smith, former staff writer for The Christophers and a resident of Greenwich, Conn., is a freelance writer and a counselor-in-training at the University of Bridgeport, Conn.

Jesus Christ Is Roots and Meaning

Father John T. Callahan

To me, Jesus Christ does not mean ANY-thing, because to me He is EVERY-thing. How can I encapsulate in three hundred words a loving Person about whom billions of words have been written, and who Himself spoke many words that were recorded?

Man has always sought roots and meaning for his life: a father, a mother, love, security, peace, freedom, immortality. All are found in Jesus Christ and His words—and ever so much more!

■ A father: "Food, shelter, clothing, your Father in heaven knows you need all these things, so do not worry." Jesus taught all of us to say, "Our Father."

■ A mother: From the Cross, Jesus said to John, "Son, behold your Mother." This has always been interpreted as addressed also to mankind.

■ Love: "God loved us first." Jesus told us to abide in His love. Two great commands he gave: "Love God totally; love your neighbor as yourself."

■ Peace: "My peace I give you, not as the world gives peace do I give it to you—and no one shall take it from you."

■ Freedom: "The truth shall make you free." And He also said, "I am the truth."

■ Immortality: "For this is the will of my Father,

that every one who sees the Son and believes in Him shall have eternal life: and I will raise him up on the last day."

■ Suffering: "Unless a man take up his cross daily, and follows Me, he is not worthy to be called My disciple."

As I approach the three-score and ten years reputedly granted to man as his lifetime, I have gathered so many proofs of the divine Providence of Jesus Christ in my life and that of many others, that disbelief is impossible.

Father Callahan is director-general of Madonna House Apostolate in Combermere, Ont., Canada.

Let It Start!

Barbara Rogers, Ph.D.

It was His patience at first that struck me, as if there had been nothing to wait for but someone saying, "Let it start!"

Like a good but dumb parent, He kept giving everything—and I kept saying I wasn't having any of that senseless generosity.

I was suspicious, even then, and He had only made overtures.

Like everyone else, I thought He must want something—and it took me some time to figure out what it was.

I had been told, always, that God was a Father, Christ a Brother, so I thought I knew what they wanted:

Sacrifice, sacrifice, being what others want—not what I am!

I had heard it before.

"Is it Your will," I retaliated, "that I become what others tell me to be? Are You one more of those others? No, no!"

I recognized the tired laughter, my own, the one I use with my children.

Then I heard Him try again:

"I want to know you, but I can't until you let it

start. See it as a dance: come, a foot here, a hand up,
in mine. Let it start!"

*Barbara Rogers is professor of literature at Ramapo
College, Mahwah, N.J.*

Shared Happiness

Sister Marie Bernadette

He is God, Son of God, made flesh out of love for His Father and out of love for men. It is this love which allowed Him to welcome death—and after what suffering! As a real Man, He suffered so much that every suffering man can now say to himself, "Jesus walked before me on this way!"

Christ is risen, He is alive today. I meet Him in the Eucharist, in the Word, in each one of my brothers and sisters, in all human beings—particularly the poorest. I meet Him in whatever happens if I know how to look with His eyes.

He enchanted me since my earliest age in a Christian home where I could see my father and mother living by their faith. When in the morning my brother, my sister and I went to Mass, we would meet Daddy who was returning from a still earlier Mass.

That is why when Jesus called me very soon to follow Him in the radicalism of love, I did not hesitate: I chose the religious life when I was nineteen. I am now seventy-two, and I have not had a single moment of regret.

In spite of my poverty, weakness, sinfulness, of which I become better aware every day, He has filled me beyond everything I could dream.

I gaze upon Him in the Gospels, and the discovery, still quite limited, of what He is, of His personal spiritual life, of His relationship with the Father and the Spirit, of His love for all men and for all of man, of His passionate desire to meet them in the midst of what is best in them, to save them—even Judas He called "my friend" at the very moment of treason—all this enchants me and moves me to encounter Him ceaselessly, so that it may no longer be "I who live, but He who lives in me." He is the marvelous All who gives absolute meaning to my life.

It is this happiness I tried to share with the young, while I myself was young, and which I dream today to share with all those whose path crosses mine. "The Lord is my Strength and my Song!" *Alleluia! Alleluia!*

Sister Marie Bernadette of Brussels, Belgium, is a retired college teacher.

Because of This...

(Cf. Phil 2:9)

Father Gerald M. Dolan, O.F.M.

I have come to know something of the language of love by looking upon the face of Jesus. The Word, incarnate from Mary the Virgin, offers Himself in the form of this language.

We no longer see Jesus walking along our streets as He did in His own place and time. There are passages in the Gospels which have convinced me that such an encounter cannot be our way of seeing the Lord He said to Philip, "Whoever has seen me has seen the Father. . . . Do you believe that I am in the Father and the Father is in me?" (John 14:9-10).

And later, we hear Him say, "A little while now and the world will see me no more; but you see me as one who has life and you will have life." (John 14:19) I see Jesus as the Obedient One whose full-hearted attention to His Father typifies the way I must journey.

Ever-focused upon the Father, He has come, and His coming has consecrated our earth and our time. He has taken flesh in the womb of a woman; He has gone down into the waters of the Jordan River, and into the grave: thereby did He communicate something of Himself, of His glory, to all that is. Because of His coming, every man's coming to life in his mother's womb is holy; our own flesh and blood, and what we take from the earth for our sustenance, water and wine, bread and oil, are holy. Even death is holy, because He is risen from the grave.

The Jesus I see is the one who moves to His Father and enters into the Holy of Holies; He moves beyond and ahead of me in the culminating act of His obedience. His is the obedience of the one who became poor that I be enriched by His poverty. His entrance into the Holy of Holies beckons me to follow, because He is the Way. And I know that His entering is not a withdrawing from His earth and mine, or from our history: His entering into the place of His Father's glory tells me that my being and my history, this earth upon which we live and from which we draw our sustenance, is redeemed and made new. In His going, I see the sense of it all: only as He goes to the Father can He be present to all men in the power of the Holy Spirit.

I do not see His features, nor do I feel the pressure of His touch. I do, however, perceive His glory with particular brilliance in the face of a child who smiles in the assurance that the world is good; I see it in the tranquility of family love, in the peace of gentle old age. There are times when it shines forth in the work of human hands: that bread of the earth and that wine of endearment—the Eucharist—which give joy and power to the faltering heart, and a glimpse of Jesus' glory as He stood before the three disciples on the holy mountain of Transfiguration.

My vision is of Jesus the Almighty One who has fulfilled in Himself, and can fulfill in the heart of each one of us, everything that can contribute to peace and justice on earth. He is Adam; He is the Man in whom we find peace. And as He enters the Holy of Holies to give all to the Father, the nail-pierced hands which sustain all and the nail-pierced feet on which He walks, make known to us the price of His gift, and show us the path we are to follow. The drama takes place now in our flesh. The journey begins now, in response to the One who, being enthroned at the right hand of the Father, is present to us in His Spirit as the One who fills all things.

Oh, to have eyes able to gaze more deeply into the marvels of His mercy! And to have a heart so centered on the glory of His face as to be transfigured into radiant power!

We cannot perceive the Lord directly with bodily sight. Yet, his presence in sacrament and word can be truly "seen." And this vision of peace is the only hope for the world.

Father Dolan, a Franciscan, is a professor at Christ the King Seminary in East Aurora, N.Y.

The Presence of God

Steve Garwood

The first Sunday after our child was born, our priest let me bring the Blessed Sacrament home to give to my wife who was still recuperating. When I got home from church, friends started dropping by to see the new baby, so I placed the pyx containing the Eucharist on our icon shelf in the living room. By the time the last visitor had left, my wife had fallen asleep. We had not yet had time alone for our eucharistic service.

On my way to bed, I turned off all the lights in the house. As I walked through the darkened living room, I felt compelled to kneel in reverence before the shelf where the Sacrament lay. My knees were on the floor, and I had bowed my head when it hit me like a shock wave: I was not alone in the room!

Have you ever been startled by someone appearing suddenly around a corner or through a door when you thought no one was there? That's how I felt. Blood pounded in my ears and all the hairs on my body stood on end. I thrust my face to the floor and spread my hands out in supplication before me.

"Lord Jesus Christ, Son of God," I said aloud, "have mercy on me an ungrateful sinner. You are here before me, in my house, and You have blessed me so much.

I'm so unworthy: have mercy on me! Lord, have mercy on us all!"

It sounds awkward as I write it, but that's exactly what I said. I felt my closed little heart torn open and flooded with love as everything within me flowed out to meet Him. I felt I could not raise my face, for if I were to see Jesus standing there in front of me, it would be too much to bear.

God knows, of course, that most of us can live but a short time on the breathless mountaintop with his unveiled presence. So after a while, my prayer faded into silence, and the overwhelming intensity of the moment diminished. I had been changed, though. God had called me to take another step closer to Him. In person, He had asked me to see Him more clearly, to know Him more deeply.

I got up, knowing that Jesus Christ is truly Emmanuel, God-With-Us!

Steve Garwood is a musician and building contractor in Columbus, S.C.

The Christ of Crisis

Brother James S. Deschene, O.S.B.

Christ is always the Unexpected One, the Disturber of my peace, the Destroyer of my illusions—the One who comes into my life and leaves it in ruins, yet who is not afraid to stay and sit with me there in my heart's ruin, quietly laying the foundations of a joy deeper than I had ever hoped possible—a joy that is mine only if I do not flee this Christ of Crisis who invades my peace and security.

I met Him once in a dream: As I enter a posh restaurant and am seated, a shabbily dressed man comes up to me muttering mad threats. No one seems to notice, though I am deeply embarrassed. He goes back to his own table, talking to himself. My own meal comes, but I cannot enjoy it as I am conscious of him sitting across the room, eating noisily.

Soon he finishes and I know he will come over to me again. What shall I do? No one is taking any notice of him or of me, apart from the waiter who fusses about the table. If I ignore this shabby man, I think he will be dangerous; yet I do not want to get really involved with him.

What I do is to greet him in a friendly way as he goes by my table. He talks, rather madly and incoherently, but in an utterly gentle and unthreatening

way. He begins to leave, putting on a grimy raincoat.
I ask him who he is.

His eyes, luminous, brown, look deeply into mine:
"I am the Suffering Servant," he says and leaves.

Through the window, I see his slightly comic, un-
gainly figure shuffling away. And I realize that—in my
craving for respectability and security—I have missed
an encounter with the Lord of Life.

*Brother Deschene is a member of the ecumenical
monks of St. Benedict at Christ-of-the-Hills Monastery
in San Antonio, Tex.*

Thank You, Lord!

Abbot Samuel Greene, O.S.B.

Since my earliest recollection, the call of Jesus Christ has been integral with the meaning of Jesus Christ in my life. In many ways, for me, that call is beautiful and terrifying: it is the call to the desert—the call to seek God and God alone. It is the call to radically live out the Gospel life in company with my brothers, whom the Lord has sent me. It is terrifying, because at the same time I know I am weak and fragile: I am a sinner, you see!

And yet, in this also there is comfort: I am continuously overwhelmed by God's loving kindness and mercy. Our God is a forgiving God. I am awestruck by His forgiveness in my life. To know you are loved without condition is a rare and forceful thing. I seek to respond to this by giving myself and my brothers more and more each day. And yet, in doing this, I fall down and pick myself up again in His loving kindness.

This perhaps is what it means to be a monk: while seeking God, to fall down and pick oneself up; to keep going, fall down and pick oneself up; to keep going, fall down and pick oneself up; and to keep going again and again. . . .

The awfulness of it is that I can continue doing this unendingly; and the fearfulness of it is how short I fall

of the mark. My fear arises from the realization that
Jesus is calling upon me to give everything—my very
self—to Him, in and through the call to community, a
call filled with the joy of brotherhood and the loneliness of the desert. It is scary to go out into the desert!

After a while, in my fear and loneliness, I have
begun slowly (and with varying degrees of consistency)
to achieve an understanding that flowers do bloom in
the desert of my heart. This flowering of new life and
continuous dying of self is the inherent experience of
Jesus Christ in my life. His call is no longer for me
an abstract intellectual appeal: it springs out of my
very guts. From the depths of my being wells up the
overwhelming need to respond to it. And so, there is
this constant on-going process of death and new life.

As I move in the waters of the spirit, opening my
clutching hands, relaxing and breathing in, deeply, His
presence in the universe, I gently become more and
more aware that this cycle is part of God's universal
flow within His creation which bears His Logos. This
process is not painless—and yet out of pain comes
growth, and more and more relaxing and letting go.

The practice of the Jesus Prayer (referred to under
many names, including the Centering Prayer,) has
enabled me to achieve a deeper sense of peace and of
reliance upon the Lord: a very deep and personal experience with my Lord, working in the world, in His
creation, in my heart, and especially, in the love I am
able to share with my brothers in Christ, and to receive from them.

As I move forward in my lonely search to seek the
face of God, I know full well my own unworthiness and

weakness; I also know His forgiveness, His love, His redeeming power; I am able to trust, to love, to be loved.

Thank you, Lord!

Abbot Greene is the head of the ecumenical monks of St. Benedict at Christ-of-the-Hills Monastery, San Antonio, Tex.

If you enjoyed this book and believe in The Christopher philosophy, here are some ways you can support the Christopher movement:

- Include The Christophers in your daily prayers.
- Introduce friends to Christopher News Notes.
- Interest young people in the Christopher idea of service.
- Become a Christopher sponsor through regular monthly contributions (details available on request).
- Mention The Christophers in your will (write for our free literature on the need to make a will).
- Watch our weekly TV program if it is shown in your area. If it is not shown locally, let station managers know that this quality programming is available to them without charge.
- Encourage editors to enquire about our inspirational columns for daily and weekly newspapers.

It is better to light one candle than to curse the darkness.

Conversations

Audiocassettes containing the full interviews from some of our most popular Christopher Closeup programs are available to individuals. People such as Cardinal Suenens and Common Cause founder John W. Gardner are among those featured. The series of 16 tapes is called Christopher Conversations. Topics discussed include prayer, child abuse, aging, alcoholism, cancer and mental health. Write for a free descriptive brochure. (The Christophers, 12 East 48th St., New York, NY 10017)

Closeup

The program is called Christopher Closeup. It provides a look at the people who are shaping tomorrow's world today. And it is one of the longest-running shows of its kind in television history.

Father James Keller launched the program in 1952. Now the co-hosts are Father John Catoir, director of The Christophers, and Jeanne Glynn, the program's executive producer.

Weekly they bring into homes throughout the country and overseas people who are demonstrating that individuals can make a difference—that they can have an impact on our times.

Make Christopher Closeup part of your viewing habits. For time and station, consult your local listings or your cablevision programming schedule. If the program is not shown in your area, contact station program directors and suggest that they add Christopher Closeup to their schedule.